Build and Grow Your HVAC BUSINESS

Greg McAfee

Build and Grow Your

HVAC BUSINESS

Greg McAfee

How I Turned $274 into a Multi-Million Dollar Company

info@braughlerbooks.com

Printed in the United States of America
Published by Braughler Books LLC., Springboro, Ohio

First printing, 2019

ISBN: 978-1-970063-14-1 soft cover
ISBN: 978-1-970063-31-8 ebook

Library of Congress Control Number: 2019942953

Ordering information: Special discounts are available on quantity purchases by bookstores, corporations, associations, and others. For details, contact the publisher at:

sales@braughlerbooks.com

or at 937-58-BOOKS

For questions or comments about this book, please write to:

info@braughlerbooks.com

Braughler™
Books
braughlerbooks.com

Advance praise for

Build and Grow Your HVAC Business
by Greg McAfee

"I'm determined that whether you are a new start-up or have been in business through multi-generations, this book is exactly what you need and I strongly endorse it."

—RON SMITH,
a crusader in the world of HVAC and best-selling author.

"Throughout this owner's growth manual, you'll find examples of how to successfully develop processes, culture and tactics along with innovative ways to differentiate and grow your business in a readily understandable, quick read format. While running a business is complex, Greg provides effective examples of how to channel your passion, create excellent customer experiences and succeed!"

—D. KELLY AMMON, CPA

Acknowledgments

Thank God for all the blessings and opportunities He's bestowed on me thus far in this life.

Thanks to my parents for giving me life, responsibilities, and discipline when I needed it.

Thanks to my wife, Naomi for all your love, support and prayers over the years and for helping to edit this book.

To my kids, Travis and Tiffany, I'm glad you were born! Never forget that with God, all things are possible. Stay focused and stay hungry!

To the McAfee Leadership Team who have stayed the course, your dedication and hard work has afforded me the time I've needed to write this book, and for that I am grateful.

Thanks to the entire McAfee team for all your hard work, for making sure we take care of our customers, and for representing the McAfee name well! Special thanks to Chris Bryant, Angie Downey, Candice Salley and Michael Graham for caring so much about the "McAfee Way" and for helping me.

Thanks to Kelly Ammon for your many years of friendship, support, and solid business advice.

Thanks to our McAfee customers for your loyalty and support and for placing your trust in us.

Contents

Contents

Preface

What you are about to read is my story. Like many of you, I don't have a business degree and attended very little college. At one time, I didn't understand a profit and loss statement or a balance sheet. However, I had a desire to build a profitable company that served the community. So I had to learn and learn fast.

Today my desire is to help you build your business so you can provide for your family, serve your community well, and enjoy the rewards of profit. By reading these pages, you will see how my success can become your success. The mistakes I learned from—well, I hope you can learn from them too.

From Firestone to Entrepreneur

"If I had eight hours to chop down a tree, I'd spend six sharpening my axe." —Abraham Lincoln

Once, I dreamt that the best possible job was to work at Firestone Tire and Rubber Company. What I learned early on, though, is that just as we change, so do our dreams and aspirations.

I was born in Akron, Ohio, and grew up in the small industrial town of Mansfield in the late 1960s and 1970s. I watched my father and grandfather build long careers in the tire factory and on the warehouse floors; there they had security, as well as an identity. They rarely missed work, and both came home reeking of rubber. Most would have found that a nearly intolerable stench, but it was the norm to hear my grandmother proclaim, *"I love that smell!"* when my grandfather walked through the door. *"It puts the bread and butter on the table,"* she gratefully declared.

I was primed to follow in their footsteps, but working at Firestone turned out to be a world away from the dream I would eventually pursue. In 1990, I followed that dream and launched McAfee Heating and Air Conditioning Company, Inc. Since then, I've worked tirelessly to build a company rooted in quality service and ethical business practices. Along the way I have developed a passion for helping other entrepreneurs follow their own dreams. Many companies either fail in their early years or just scrape by, but it doesn't have to be that way. We shouldn't allow our dreams to stop at the first struggle and remain small.

I have extensively studied my business and how we blossomed from our humble roots to become an award-winning, multimillion-dollar, successful small business. In my analysis, I have come to recognize the key principles that have guided our growth:

- Be strategic
- Be teachable
- Be a leader
- Be well known
- Be giving
- Be innovative
- Be passionate
- Be disruptive
- Be ready

Throughout the following chapters, we will walk through each of these principles with examples from my business and from other successful entrepreneurs who have also followed their dreams.

From Firestone to Entrepreneur

I spent my childhood working odd jobs: delivering papers, selling vegetables door to door, picking apples, and even washing Dad's car in trade for driving it up and down the driveway at age thirteen. High school was so boring to me that I absolutely couldn't wait to throw my mortarboard in the air and get out of there. I had two jobs during my high school years and enjoyed working.

Due to my distaste for the academics, I graduated with a low GPA. Thus, when a job opened at a new Firestone facility in Dayton, Ohio, I jumped at the opportunity to follow my Firestone dream, and at nineteen, I loaded my pickup truck with a bed, a chair, and the few other things I could call my own and headed to Dayton.

I wasn't familiar with the area, but I was excited about the opportunity to move. It was the early 1980s, and industry was thriving. I couldn't wait to become a third-generation Firestone employee; to follow in my father's and grandfather's steel-toed boot-steps!

Like my Dad, I arrived well before starting time almost every morning. Most of the time I drove a forklift and entertained myself by trying to see how fast I could load or unload thousands of pounds of tires in a day. Other times, I manually loaded and unloaded truck trailers. Talk about hard work! In the summer the warehouse and semitrailers smoldered at over 120 degrees, and in the winter the mercury was lucky to hit ten, but either way I forged ahead as quickly as I could, always trying to beat my own record of productivity. At Firestone, the department supervisor ventured around every afternoon to offer overtime. Many refused, but I rarely turned it down. Unfortunately, this was not an acceptable concept in a unionized workplace. Maybe working hard and fast was not the best way to win friends, but I am sure I influenced many by my efforts anyway. For a short time I even had the warehouse manager posting goals and records on a bulletin board.

Because my work ethic wasn't the norm and didn't sit well with my coworkers, the idea fizzled out. What a shame! As the late Zig Ziglar once said, *"What you get by achieving your goals is not as important as what you become by achieving your goals."* I can't imagine how my business would function today if we did not set goals, push hard to break records and encourage others to do the same. I was, and still am, grateful for the opportunity to work at Firestone, and for the experience I learned there.

About three years into the job, though, I had an epiphany when I caught a glimpse of a much older forklift driver moving tires around the warehouse. As I watched him toil, something dawned on me: *I don't want to spend the rest of my life doing this.* As much as I thought I was living my dream, I knew I didn't want to be that man some thirty years later. My dream changed, and I knew something new and different had to be out there. I just needed to find it.

I did find something, at least temporarily, via a stint in the United States Marine Corps (USMC). Back in high school, a friend had tried to get me to join under the Marines Buddy Enlistment Program, but I didn't at the time. Still a lingering idea, I decided my best option to get off that forklift was to become one of the few and the proud.

I enlisted in the USMC in the mid-1980s, attended basic training at Parris Island, and got stationed at Twentynine Palms, California. After that, I served in the USMC Reserves, stationed in a Communications Company, Fourth Marine Division, near Cincinnati, Ohio. Back in Dayton, Firestone held my position during my military service, so upon discharge I soon found myself working there full-time yet again, only this time I also served in the Reserves one weekend each month.

The Marines equipped me well for business, and during my enlistment I learned many traits that have helped me along the way and sharpened my leadership skills. As anyone who served knows, many of the tasks in the military are menial, but today I understand why we were taught a specific way to pick up trash and to march in squads to the mess hall a certain way. For a Marine, success in leadership is just one stripe away, and we always understood what it took to earn that stripe. Of course, I learned methods to be more disciplined and structured, and from day one the Marines instilled in me a love for competition.

Boot camp was full of challenges many could not perform prior to arriving. One was the daunting Crucible Confidence Course. In the third and final phase of boot camp, we spent fifty-four hours working and hiking with little to no sleep. During the Confidence Course, we encountered a series of fifteen strenuous obstacles. Getting through Crucible week meant we made it and would become United States Marines, so most of us gave it our all. Mind you, up until then, we were just recruits, and those in the Corps know this was putting it nicely.

Many months after the completion of boot camp, I had an opportunity to take some classes. One I chose randomly was a refrigeration course, recalling my dad's rare but sage advice that I should someday go into heating, ventilating, and air conditioning (HVAC). *"There will always be work,"* he said, and I never forgot that. I now know just how right he was!

After my service in the Marines, I enrolled in an HVAC night class at the county adult vocational school. By that time, my dad had transferred and was working for Firestone in Dayton, and he took the class with me. In that classroom, a seed was planted, and my dream began to change once again. As I sat there listening and learning, I knew I'd own my own business someday. Even though I had no idea how or when it would happen, the vision became very clear to me. I daydreamed about it as I worked days at Firestone, since driving a forklift around leaves a lot of time to fill one's head. Call it wishful thinking, but as I dreamt of owning my own business and continued taking HVAC classes, I had business cards made with my name on one side and my Dad's on the other.

Wisely, my instructor urged me to get some hands-on experience before launching out on my own. Thank goodness I heeded his advice when I took my leap of faith. I left my job at Firestone after being hired on as a helper at a small heating company in a Dayton suburb; a move that represented a substantial pay cut. I saw it as a risk, but stepping away from Firestone was really just a stepping-stone that carried me that much closer to the fulfillment of my dream.

Today, I have the privilege and opportunity to teach others, including many youth. I always challenge young people to resist the urge to go after the big bucks too soon; rather, they must earn their way up the ladder and learn all they can along the way. In my own journey, I discovered that my willingness to work for less pay brought greater gain. Sure, it was a risky venture, but little did I realize, that the initial pay reduction could reap such big dividends later.

I worked for that little company for nine months before the owner decided to let me go. *"You'll never make it as a mechanic,"* he said, not even bothering to try softening the blow. I was devastated and embarrassed, but in the end he was right. I wasn't the best mechanic, but I found out pretty fast what I am good at. Those nine months paid off because I learned a lot about what *not* to do in business. One important lesson was that working *in* your business without working *on* it would only get you so far. Another thing I realized was that acting as if you cannot afford to advertise is small thinking, and small thinking will keep your business just that: small.

After my "layoff," I took a job with another HVAC company, where I started as a service technician. During my experience there, I discovered that I have a knack for selling. The paper route and vegetable route paid off as they both helped me get used to talking to people door to door. I actually got so good at sales that many months in a row, I outsold their full-time salesperson. I continued to work there while big changes came in my personal life—namely, marrying my wife, Naomi. We had a very small wedding and honeymooned an hour away in Columbus, Ohio. We went all out for sure, but we were also wisely saving to purchase our first home, which we did that same year.

Soon thereafter, I found myself out of a job again. I should have seen the familiar signs and red flags in that company: little advertising, negative mentality, and the acceptance of mediocrity. The owner was also pocketing any profits rather than investing them back into the business. These were just more valuable lessons that later helped me in my own business. The company closed its doors six months later.

Naomi's full-time job covered most of our bills, so even though I had hoped to stay on there to bolster my experience, we decided as a couple that it was as good a time as any to take the chance and launch my own business. Just like that, my dream was underway. It happened far sooner than we planned, but it was time to give that dream of mine some real wings and pray it would take off!

· · · · ·

I did not have a huge nest egg to throw into my start-up. After all, we had just gotten married and bought a house. In fact, all I really had was the meager $274 in my bank account and a used Ford Ranger, ironically lacking air conditioning. In spite of the lack of any substantial capital, I took the leap, put my shingle out, and proudly opened McAfee Heating and Air Conditioning Co., Inc.

It was a very slow process, but it did open my eyes to the reality that impatience can be a virtue, too, at least in business. I have never enjoyed waiting on anything, so I preferred not to make my customers wait. I adopted a sense of urgency that still holds strong today. We are able to respond quickly and get jobs done fast without cutting any corners.

On the flipside, another learning opportunity for me was that I had to wait to grow. Most founders assume they can hit the ground running, but what I discovered is that slow growth has its advantages. I spent days combing through a crisscross directory phone book (an ancient resource before entrepreneurs had access to the internet). I made plenty of phone calls and went street to street, knocking on doors to pitch my services. It was not easy, and it often took a few hundred meetings and phone calls before anyone agreed to let me perform a service call or a system tune-up.

When I wasn't making calls, I drove my little Ford Ranger to countless retail stores. I asked to speak with the managers of the fledgling establishments then posed one simple question: *"Have you had your heating and air system serviced lately?"* Every so often, this led to some work, such as a filter or belt replacement. I completed those projects working out of our home, a small ranch house in Beavercreek, a suburb of Dayton.

Unlike me, my wife has always been very patient, and she supported me in many ways. Naomi graciously allowed me to slather our kitchen cabinets with sticky notes that eventually became my weekly schedule. Although it was not the most pleasing décor, I think she was just happy to see that I actually had some work on the board—or at least on the cupboard!

Those days felt long and a little lonely. I recall feeling some guilt, and I never wanted to be home when Naomi came home from work. Sometimes, I even drove around for a half-hour before pulling into the driveway after she returned. I didn't want her to feel like I was slacking.

I'll never forget one particularly worrisome time when the phone didn't ring for two weeks. That might not have been so bad if it was my first year in business, but this was during my second year. *"Do you think this is going to work, Greg? Maybe you should get a real job,"* some people had the gumption to say, and I'm sure everyone else was thinking it even if they didn't say it. Nevertheless, I kept chugging away, driving my truck around with the McAfee logo plastered on the side.

In the early 1990s I didn't know much about Steve Jobs, but now I know how right he was when he said, *"I'm convinced that about half of what separates successful entrepreneurs from the non-successful ones is pure perseverance."* Around that time, someone said to me, *"I see your trucks everywhere!"* Wow! I thought, and that was just the motivation I needed. I was so excited and knew I was making progress, especially since I had only one truck. That truck had a service cap and ladder on top, which allowed me to do jobs right away, but often I chose to schedule non-emergency appointments out a day or two. I assumed that if I appeared busier than I actually was, clients would have more confidence in me. I wanted everyone to think I was in high demand to see more value in hiring me.

Perception is everything, and I do mean everything! Somehow, even in my first few years, I understood that, and it still helps us today. We've built such a solid brand that many think we're ten times bigger than we are. And to think, it all started with one little logo on the side of one little truck!

After wearing out many pairs of shoes while marketing door-to-door, I finally caught a nice break and contracted with a home warranty company. I needed my truck to be in driveways and McAfee stickers needed to show up on furnaces. Working with the home warranty company helped me do just that. Soon I was scheduling ten to fifteen more service calls a week.

There were many reasons I chose to end my contract with the home warranty company after only one year, but those twelve months did make a significant impact on my business and really gave me the kick-start I needed. Today, I advise new businesses to try aligning with home warranty companies, but they should be just that: a kick-start. Do not rely or depend on another business to grow yours.

To be a successful start-up in any field, you must know when to pull the plug on initiatives. I never turned down any work the first year, but that eventually became very draining. Thus, after a year with that home warranty company, it was time to make the leap into becoming a viable business with higher margins.

* * * * *

When my business was in its infancy, it was treated as just that: a baby. When it was newborn to ten years old, it required much more care and attention. In other words, I would not consider leaving it alone to take a long vacation or go hunting, fishing, or camping for two weeks. It had to be cared for, nurtured, and loved. Yes, you must love what you do. After all, if *you* aren't passionate about its growth, who will be?

We did a few critical things right from the get-go, including setting ourselves up as a professional business. I was blessed to have assistance from my sister-in-law, a diligent bookkeeper who made sure we logged our expenses, recorded all income, and paid our taxes. Today, I give this same advice to the business owners I coach.

Because of those early monthly financial statements, which she ensured were accurate, I learned to enjoy reviewing reports and learned the basic of metrics. Whether out of disorganization or deception, businesses that try to skimp on accounting will eventually suffer for it. Get your books in order, know what you are looking at and why, and pay your taxes from the start. You'll be glad you did, but on the contrary, you probably won't be around long if you don't.

Early on, I did work for an accountant, Mr. Kentner, who gave me expert advice to pay myself a set salary. Up to that point, during my first year of business, I didn't take any pay at all, other than an occasional draw of fifty bucks here and there. He encouraged me to begin paying myself right away and to never waver from it. Like many of you, we didn't think we could afford to pay ourselves, but we did. Billionaire Mark Cuban has said, "*Only morons start a business off of a loan,*" and rightly so. Statistics show that most successful start-ups begin with more elbow grease, sweat, and tears than with borrowed money. Mr. Kentner suggested that I pay myself as we would pay a supplier, always in full and always on time. We heeded his advice and started with a $1,200 monthly salary, which gradually increased every six months. As it turned out, his counsel was wise and what I needed to hear at that time. I have shared it with many start-up businesses.

We also managed to avoid debt. Although we established credit lines with our suppliers, we paid them off monthly. As mentioned, we grew very slowly, which made it possible to avoid borrowing; however, the growth we did experience brought about a need for more people and company vehicles. By the end of our third year in business, I was prepared to place a down payment on my first new truck and finance the remainder. I let someone else drive the Ford Ranger, and passing down vehicles became a tradition that has continued. To this day, certain team members cannot wait for me to get a new vehicle, because they love those almost new hand-me-downs!

Aside from a few short lines of credit, which we paid off quickly, we purchased only what we could afford. In fact, I didn't even take our first full line of credit for nine years. By keeping our debt low, we've experienced freedom and stayed in business. We even remained debt free when we moved out of the kitchen and constructed the garage behind our house.

The garage was twenty-four feet by twenty-four feet, half of which was used for office and the other half for warehouse. We were thrilled to have a space to work from outside our home, but it still wasn't easy. The garage had no plumbing, so our first receptionist had to walk to the house to use the restroom and the remainder of our team had to make pit stops elsewhere. The garage also lacked privacy. When I needed to have confidential meetings with team members, everyone had to leave the office. In spite of our one-room office and our lack of indoor plumbing, we somehow managed to do almost a million dollars in sales the final year we operated from that little garage.

Because we could only squeeze so many in a one-room office, a lack of space kept us from increasing our sales and office staff. Seeing this early enough and planning for the future was critical. After six years in the garage, we bought a three-acre tract in a business area just fifteen minutes from our home. A year later, once the land purchase was paid in full, we constructed an 11,000-square-foot building. Unbelievably, that building actually collapsed to the ground during construction, but again, we persevered.

Still trying to plan, we thought the building would be more affordable if we leased the front portion to another business, so we looked for someone to occupy and use the space. However, to our surprise and shock, it sat vacant for eighteen months. Leasing that space remained in our prayers due to the struggle to pay the mortgage. In the end, leasing it made it all worthwhile, and we obviously survived.

Nevertheless, the stress of such overwhelming debt reinforced why debt hadn't been part of our culture in the first place. Today, we are 100 percent debt free, and that includes business, buildings, trucks, personal home, and pretty much everything— literally the kitchen sink! Debt freedom is true freedom; we are financially free. Don't get me wrong: loans are necessary at times and I'm not afraid to borrow and leverage when I need to, but I encourage all to eliminate debt as soon as possible. Reliance on credit and loans has become a way of life for many businesses, but debt should be a vehicle for growth with full intent to get out of it as soon as possible.

Cash is King: Mark Swepston

After being in this business for over forty-five years, it would appear to be common sense that everyone understands the need for good cash flow. Unfortunately, based on available statistics, this is not the case!

It is easy to be lulled to sleep by paying attention to your cash position when the U.S. market is as strong as it has been over the past ten years. We hear more about the need for skilled labor than worrying about cash. We have also enjoyed very low interest rates over the past decade, making the cost of money less of a priority. In December of 1980, inflation was out of control, and the Prime Rate hit 21.5%. It was almost impossible then for small business owners to borrow money. We may not see that high of a rate again in our lifetimes, but it's just a matter of time before the cost of money increases again. Consistently following good business practices will keep us from having to worry about it.

Growing sales can hide a lot of sins in a company. In fact, the companies that are growing fast are often the fastest to go under, due to a wide range of issues: underbidding, improperly managing jobs, the lack of good purchase order, inventory, or accounts receivable systems, to name a few. They collect money in the early stages of growth, but the jobs end up costing more than their selling price. Having better systems and controls in place would have helped save them from the crash and burn.

A husband and wife team I knew successfully grew a business, only to see it tank due to misuse of credit cards. She was the real business operator, but he quit his job to help out. Along the way, he started using supplier credit, while also incurring credit card debt, but didn't tell her the true amount owed. I was asked to review their company to see if I could help. After a couple conversations, he finally admitted that they were over $136,000 in debt, owing the majority to credit cards. Some simple math revealed that they had lost $316 daily since their grand opening. Sadly, their marriage fell apart along with their business.

My philosophy is this: Allow the size of the jobs to grow with you. For a cash flow advantage, seek smaller jobs that require a day or less to complete and can be collected upon before leaving the job. Suppliers can also help; in most cases, they will set up a line of credit, but it's a better idea to have the money in hand to pay it off within two to six weeks after purchase. If one is smart, they can grow and be very profitable with essentially a cash business, regardless of size. Of course, this is harder to accomplish as jobs get bigger and take longer. The key is to be sure the customer understands YOUR PAYMENT/COLLECTION procedures and agrees to them before starting any work. Again, payment at completion is best, but bigger jobs must be invoiced sooner than later.

Some factors are beyond your control, especially when people do not pay. We know of one general contractor whose business grew too fast, and they were thrown off a multimillion-dollar job due to lack of performance. Ultimately, without any prior announcement to their subcontractors, they had to close their doors. One subcontractor I spoke with said that as soon as he found they were shutting down a job his company was working on, he went straight to their office, only to find seventeen other subs in line, trying to collect money. Of course, no one would even open the door. How many thousands or possibly hundreds of thousands of loss can one absorb?

Some simple rules to follow:

Know your cash position EVERY DAY!

This is easy, so there's no excuse. Just follow these steps:

1. Check your bank balance online.
2. Check any credit card balances daily; most will notify you of every charge.
3. Know what bills need to be paid, including payroll and taxes
4. Know your Accounts Receivable situation

Size of company doesn't matter.

If you're small, learn how to do it yourself. It should take less than fifteen minutes a day if you keep it simple. As you grow, you will have less time, so hire a competent bookkeeper, accountant, or controller to gather this information and other financials that you need to know daily.

We recommend that at least 10 percent of your annual sales should be in cash or a cash equivalent.

Use self-maintenance agreements AND require deposits!

Work toward ensuring that at least 25 percent of your annual business is paid for in advance via maintenance agreements and job deposits. Being paid in advance is the Holy Grail of the successful HVAC/plumbing business.

Collect before leaving each job.

If you have a primarily commercial business, the invoice should always be in the customer's hand no later than twenty-four hours within completion of the work. Better yet, request credit card payment at completion from as many commercial customers as possible. Many will comply! Remember that there will be fees involved if you accept credit cards, so build that into your cost; give a "cash discount" to entice customers to pay another way. Good, professional people expect to pay and will, in a timely manner. The only people who seem to object cause additional problems later, in addition to slow payment.

—*Mark Swepston*, CEO, Atlas Butler

Much of my personal business philosophy is the product of the first business book I read, *Business by the Book*, by Larry Burkett. From then until now, his financial guidance has helped many Christian businesspeople build their enterprises on Biblical principles. He advocated keeping debt low, paying suppliers and employees before paying yourself, and remembering that a good name is worth more than great riches. I clung to those teachings in the beginning, and I still adhere to them today. Why? Because I believe in them, they've worked well, and they have proven true time and time again for us and others. The late Billy Graham said it best: *"If a person gets his attitude toward money straight, it will help straighten out almost every other area in his life."* One of those areas is certainly in business.

As all businesses do, we had to experience learning through trial and error. Many times, it was trial by fire, as we surely didn't do everything right the first time. My list of mistakes is very long, especially in hiring. I was so excited that anyone wanted to work for us that I didn't do my due diligence, such as background and drug checks. Imagine finding out that an employee you just sent to a customer's home is uninsurable or has a criminal record. I also added a few business ventures that were not good fits for McAfee, and I held on to them for too long.

In addition to all that, I attempted to do many of the daily tasks of running the business, including some I clearly was not qualified to do. Today, from reading the book *The E-Myth*, it pertains to working *on* your business rather than working *in* your business. Another mistake was being so insistent on keeping my debt low that I didn't establish enough credit for when I needed it. When I applied for a loan to construct the new building, I was rejected by five banks. Although many entrepreneurs would have given up, the sixth bank finally approved me for a loan.

We were also very *re*active in those days, rather than *pro*active. I'll share more about this in Chapter Eight, but this really hurt us in the slower months. We stared at the phone, desperately hoping it would ring, even picking it up at times to make sure it still had a dial tone. Today we call customers, which helps fill the schedule farther ahead, even in slow months. We also waited too long to invest in a computerized scheduling system, as we relied on an old-fashioned appointment book for the first twelve years of business. *"Who's got the book?"* was a regular shout around the office.

Today, having learned from all these mistakes, we meet often to discuss any necessary changes and updates. There are many benefits to being first to market with a new idea or concept, so being open to these ideas is important. Fortunately, we were able to avoid any catastrophic mistakes and instead learned from the ones we did make.

According to the US Department of Commerce, more than a million new businesses open in this country annually, but nearly 50 percent of them fail in the first year. Within five years, about 20 percent are still in business. Sadly, within a decade, only 5 percent remain. Why is this? Because many companies spend much of their energy on simply surviving rather than investing in growing and thriving.

. . . . .

You are probably wondering two things: First, what is my best tip for growing a successful family-based business? Second, how long will it take to be successful?

A business is more successful if there is good communication at home. Does your spouse want to work with you? Where do you both want to be in three, five, or ten years? As your business grows and changes, it's wise to revisit and talk through these issues often. Making these tough discussions initially can save pain and heartache later, both personally and professionally. Today I advise spouses who are involved in the business to participate in conference calls together with me during our coaching sessions.

Many of the younger business owners I coach ask, *"How long will it take for my business to really take off?"* This is difficult to say, and there are a multitude of variables, but much depends on demographics. In other words, if you are in a very hot and humid area, an HVAC start-up will likely grow faster than it would in the Midwest. It took about eight years for my business to reach an obvious upturn, but I've coached some in southern Florida who have hit high revenue numbers within the first four years of business—twice as fast as we did.

The world has changed since my father and grandfather were able to build middle-class lives for themselves and their families on the factory floor, even since I ran a forklift at Firestone. One thing that hasn't changed is the philosophy that hard work and persistence pays off. The good news is that the American dream of starting and running a successful business is still alive and as strong as it's ever been.

One last note before you dive in: This book is a very simple and quick read. After all, I'm just a furnace guy, not a great American novelist! With that in mind, remember that the principles, ideas, plans, systems, and risk-taking actions I recommend are not easy nor simple to execute. Perseverance is key, so read on and persevere! Good luck!

CHAPTER ONE

Be Strategic

"Leaders establish the vision for the future and set the strategy for getting there." —John P. Kotter

Children are prolific dreamers, driven by curiosity, imagination, and boundlessness. If you ask any five-year-old what he or she wants to be when they grow up, you can expect a variety of big-dream answers: teacher, police officer, firefighter, nurse, doctor, professional sports hero, NASCAR driver, or president! A child's mind races with lofty notions, backed by hope and limitless goals. Grownups, on the other hand, like to dismiss these thoughts as naïve or childish.

Unfortunately, for many, the dreaming spirit fades as they age and take on more responsibilities. They fear failure and rejection, become impatient and feel jaded and disgruntled. They can actually become prisoners of the daily grind and get too comfortable with the status quo, sometimes not even knowing what dreams are and forgetting they had them in the first place. Most often, this is due to fear of failure and unwillingness to risk planting the dream seed so it can grow into reality.

As American educator and minister Benjamin E. Mays said, *"The tragedy in life doesn't lie in not reaching your goal. The tragedy lies in having no goal to reach."*

At McAfee, we do our best to educate people so they see value in working within the trade. Trade jobs are very much in demand and now pay very well.

When I started McAfee Heating and Air, my dream was simple: to work for myself. In time I dreamt of building a garage to work from and later moving out of that garage and into a professional building. I haven't stopped dreaming! Today, I dream of continuing to build the best team possible and continuing to dominate our market. Being willing to be a little childlike when it comes to dreaming and always having your dream in mind will keep you ahead of most!

Be Strategic

Every dream, no matter how small or audacious, must be backed by strategy or it simply will not take flight. Being strategic has been the key factor in the growth of McAfee Heating and Air. As we have grown, we have become strategic in our operations. Year after year, we refine our goals and get better at pursuing them. The goal that got me where I am today will not carry me to where I want to go tomorrow.

Turning a dream into a reality requires multiple things. It takes time and a place to dream. It requires hard work to develop a roadmap. Perhaps the most crucial requirement is the perseverance to stay focused and confirm that you are heading in the right direction to meet the goals you have set.

Finding Time to Dream

To pursue your dream, you must set aside time to think. Most people pack their days so full that there is little time left, if any, to meditate on their business or their lives. He didn't have a cellphone, a computer, or a television, but Thomas Edison still said, *"There is no expedient to which a man will not resort to avoid the labor of thinking."* This expression is also attributed to a prominent English painter, Joshua Reynolds. Even in their day, they knew a thing or two about distractions and the damage they caused.

Today, our thirty-thousand-square-foot facility includes an Idea Center. It's a place to brainstorm and think of the next idea. A corner of the room is also designed specifically for thinking and dreaming; I call it the Retro Room due to the nostalgic furniture. The only things I ever take in there are my *Leadership Bible,* a notepad, and a pen. I want nothing to distract me, so I never, ever take the phone with me. I'm there for peace, quiet, and uninterrupted time to really think about my business and life. I ask myself important questions: *Where are we going? How do we get there? What can I do better? How can I get out of my own way?*

Business is founded on thought. Determination and enthusiasm are valuable, but thinking and dreaming are what keep us moving forward. I always leave the Idea Center with all the fodder I need for the nitty-gritty planning that comes with setting goals and mapping out the path I need to take to meet or exceed them.

Mapping Your Strategy: The Importance of Strategic Planning

What is strategic planning? It starts with knowing your company: its strengths, weaknesses, opportunities, and threats. It also reflects an understanding of the environment in which you compete: your customers, suppliers, competitors, and market trends. Once you know who and what you are, then you can start planning where to go and how to get there. This vital leadership tool will boldly direct your company toward reaching your vision. In one word, it's a *process*.

Like many of you, I operated McAfee for several years without a strategic plan or any processes in place. Even after I spent money to develop a plan, I didn't know how to use it properly, so it idly collected dust in a desk drawer. Looking back, I realize that some of the mistakes we made might have been avoided if we had weighed those decisions against the goals set forth in our strategic plan. For example, we acquired a dead-end chimney-cleaning business, but chimney cleaning was never our goal.

A strategic plan can be as easy as setting goals and then figuring out how and when you can reach them. The first step is to create a vision for your company—where you see yourself in six months to three years from now. The next step is to create a plan for getting there. You must decide how many people and how much money you will require and what resources you will need.

Nowadays we revisit our strategic plan annually. This yearly realignment helps us avoid minor and serious missteps, all while keeping me on track with my dream.

Example: Your goal is to do a million dollars in your service department

Let's say you now have three technicians averaging $150,000 in revenue per truck, and growth has been 20 to 25 percent a year. In order to reach a million, you need to know how many technicians you will need. You should be able to add a tech every ten to fourteen months, but you must plan for enough training time.

Strategy Projection: Hit the goal in four years.

Writing a Plan

There are many valuable books and websites that teach business owners how to write strategic plans, such as *How to Write a Business Plan* by Alex Genadinik. Talk to other entrepreneurs or hire a competent business coach to help you get started. While I won't spend much time on the mechanics of writing a plan, I want to share four steps of strategic planning that have been critical for my company:

- Analysis
- Mission Statement
- Action Plan
- Execution

Analysis

To know what your plan should be, you must first analyze your business, the industry, your market, and any other trends that may influence the future of your company. At times, I invite my board of advisors, leadership team, and outside consultants to a McAfee strategic planning session. Assembling a board of advisors will challenge you to stretch, and it will provide fresh perspectives, answers, and solutions that you and your team can't deliver alone. It's best to choose board members who are *not* like you.

Our strategic planning sessions are often daylong meetings away from the office. I share my vision of the company's future and we converse about it. We discuss and research our competition, demographics, and any perceived challenges. We always perform or update our SWOT (strengths, weaknesses, opportunities, and threats) analysis, a common and effective business practice.

SWOT analysis has saved McAfee from costly mistakes. For example, at one time, having our own sheet metal shop was listed as an opportunity on our SWOT analysis. Nevertheless, as we started to outgrow the capacity of the sheet metal shop we used, the lack of ability to fabricate our own sheet metal was quickly recognized as a weakness. As we planned to part ways from the sheet metal shop, our strong sense of urgency became real. We had three options: find another shop interested in growing, purchase an existing shop that had a similar culture and kept its employees, or start one from scratch. We chose the third option, so we could maintain our level of growth, our culture, and with the same sense of urgency. Had we not kept a critical eye on that part of our business, we could have been hit with a major delay in the fabrication of sheet metal and a loss of installations. Instead, we created a profitable new business that fit nicely into our overall plan. Not only can we use the shop for our own sheet metal needs, but it also has become a revenue source.

Mission and Vision Statement

Do you have a mission statement and a vision statement? If so, do your current mission and vision statements fit your company today? Will your present mission take you into tomorrow? If not, it's time to craft a new one. We review our mission and vision statements annually to make sure they still fit our plan.

A mission statement is a brief description of a company's fundamental purpose. It should answer the question, *"Why does your business exist?"* The mission statement expresses the company's purpose both for those internally and externally.

At McAfee, our mission statement is *"Leading in air quality, one home at a time."* A vision statement gives the company direction because it is about what the company wants to become. It's about dreams and aspirations and it moves the business ahead. Our vision is to be recognized as an innovator and leader in indoor air quality and to be a total home environment expert.

To help you understand how this reflects our dream for the business, let's break our mission down word for word:

"LEADING": We want to dominate our residential market. We don't want to be just another mediocre business. We want to *lead*.

"AIR QUALITY": This encompasses all parts of heating and air. Using this phrase broadens what we do to include heating, cooling, filtration, and air purification.

"ONE HOME AT A TIME": Ninety-seven percent of our business is residential, so a home is referenced in our mission statement. This part of our statement also reminds our customers and us that we are committed to taking care of EACH customer's needs thoroughly, promptly, and with quality; one home at a time.

A mission statement should be short and to the point so it is easy for every team member to commit to memory. The mission statement keeps us focused on the work we do best. Anyone in our company can recite it to you. It's that ingrained in our culture. The entire strategic plan should underpin this mission.

Action Plan

With your mission statement in place, you can put in motion the steps to meet it. The action plan is how those strategic goals will be accomplished. It can include tactics, responsibilities, timelines, and budgets—all the practical steps to reaching your dream.

The action plan details what needs to happen to reach each goal. For example, what would it take to grow by 15 percent in the next year? First, you may need to increase your advertising and marketing budget. If you have a good, solid marketing plan, this will help create a demand. When that phone begins ringing with new or repeat business, you may need to hire more people, purchase more vehicles, and add or promote another manager or two to the team. This requires careful planning.

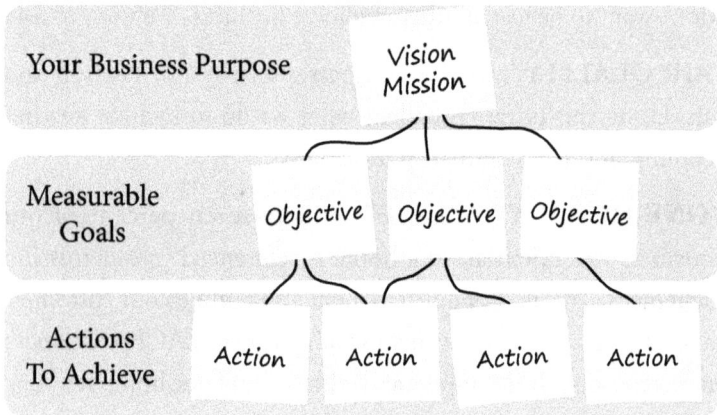

Your Business Purpose	Vision Mission
Measurable Goals	Objective Objective Objective
Actions To Achieve	Action Action Action Action

Your action plan sets forth the specific steps you need to take to meet your goals. It is the key to becoming proactive instead of reactive. This part of your planning helps to shape the day-to-day work of your leadership team.

You can create a task list and action items, team goals to revisit at team meetings, and individual goals to discuss at one-on-one meetings. It's a good idea to use the SMART goal-setting format:

Specific **M**easurable **A**chievable **R**ealistic **T**imely

Executing Your Plan

Putting your plan in writing is a good start, but you will then need to take it to the next level. It is just as important to actively follow and fine-tune a strategy after all the major writing and planning is complete. Would you take the time to write out a grocery list but never pull it out of your pocket at the store? You might remember most of your groceries, but you would be frustrated and likely not have enough food for the week, not to mention, wasting your money on things you shouldn't have been shopping for in the first place. Following the plan will help you avoid these issues in your business, as well as in the grocery aisle!

Having a strong strategic plan for your dream is freeing; it makes your lofty goals achievable. That, in turn, will allow you to dream and accomplish bigger dreams than you ever thought possible.

CHAPTER TWO

Be Teachable

"Listen to advice and accept instruction, and in the end you will be wise." —Proverbs 19:20 (NIV)

I'd like to share two ways that my business grew. The first was hiring a business coach, which I was advised to do and did within the first few years of business, and the second was when some very successful friends recommended forming a board of advisors.

Board of Advisors

In June 2007, I was encouraged by a few mentors to form a board of advisors. I assembled three people whose knowledge in business compensated for areas in which I knew I was weak. We must listen to the wisdom of others and not rely only on what we think we know. My board was interested in my success, and at times, were willing to push me beyond my own capabilities. Our first meeting was both exciting and scary. I gladly shared my story with them to help them understand my business and they had many questions for me. Certainly, it was a draining experience, but it was challenging, and I knew it would change the course of my business.

For that counsel to prove beneficial and take shape, I had to be teachable and humble, open to their wisdom. There was no room for ego. Therefore, I walked into that board meeting with a teachable spirit and broad shoulders. I encouraged them to be tough on me, to question my thought process and challenge my decisions, and let me tell you, they sure followed through with that!

That board of advisors would have been of little value if I had constantly taken a defensive stance, and that would have been frustrating for them as well. Maintaining a teachable spirit has been a key component of my business success.

I have the privilege of coaching many leaders today. Several say they want to learn, but few want to listen. Learning comes from a variety of sources: continuing education, mentors, your staff, your customers, books and resources, industry leaders, and business coaches. Reading hundreds of business books is great, but if you are not open to really learning from what the authors have to say, it would be of no value.

The Importance of Creating an Advisory Board

Setting up a board was critical to some changes and advancements we've made over the past several years. Clay Mathile, former owner of the well-known Iams pet nutrition company, said *"I would not open a popcorn stand in Courthouse Square without setting up an advisory board first."* It's just that important.

Finding the Right Advisors

You may think you already have this issue under control, that you have good people and don't need any help, not internally and certainly not from outsiders. Perhaps you think boards are for bigger companies. Maybe you want to ask, "How in the world can I attract or afford people with any interest in my small outfit?"

Believe me; I thought the same way once. However, if you really want your business to accelerate, you may want to reconsider. Well-known motivator and self-development author Brian Tracy said it well: *"You can make excuses, or you can make progress. You choose."*

Like all decisions in business, selecting a board of advisors requires careful thought. Consider different advisors for different areas of expertise. What are your weaknesses? Do you struggle with finances, marketing, team building, human resources, strategic planning, or operations? Remember that your outside board members should be people who are *not* like you. Choose those who have strengths that will offset your weak areas. Consider selecting well-known or retired successful business leaders in your area.

One of my board members was just that, a successful owner of a leading national home improvement company. Another was a human resources expert who assisted in most of the hiring for a large corporation. My third was a former owner of a manufacturing company, someone who specialized in developing core operations of business. I've also been served well by some great mentors in my industry, and I still rely on them when it comes to industry-specific matters. Although I value and respect them, I know the things that work for their companies won't necessarily be suitable for mine. A board of advisors brings new, fresh ideas that will fit *your* company. I strive for originality and challenge others to be original too. Of course, it's okay to R&D (rob and duplicate) certain ideas, but you must tweak those ideas to make them fit you. At McAfee, most all of our plans are homegrown.

I hope that you maintain good working relationships with your vendors, banker, attorney, and accountant, but I don't recommend that any of these hold positions on your board. Why? Put simply, a potential board member should have no conflict of interest, no desire to promote or generate income for their firm. Rather, their number-one aim should be to help your company perform at a higher level.

Don't discount these, however, as excellent resources who may identify prospects for your board. Consider, too, that some brilliant and insightful baby boomers are retiring by the millions now. Many do not require part-time jobs for the money as much as they desire the feeling of being needed. Helping your small business grow may be just the purpose they require!

Frequently Asked Questions (FAQs) About Starting a Board of Advisors

How many people should serve on my board?
Three, on average, and no more than four.

How much should I pay?
Depending on the size of your company, payment for board members ranges from $400 to $1,000 per meeting. However, good board members don't serve for the purpose of making money. If they have an asking price up front, I recommend you don't use them. Your payment is just to show appreciation.

How often should we meet?
Three to four times a year is recommended.

Should I have a contract with each member?
Yes! A two-year contract makes it easy enough for someone to leave the board if they need to. Be sure to include an attendance policy in the contract. With a small board it's important that

everyone is able to attend. If one of my board members can't make a meeting, we reschedule, because each member is that important.

Where should we meet?
Find a nice, neutral space. Your CPA or attorney may allow you to use or rent their conference room. The chamber of commerce or an industry association you belong to may have facilities you can use. If a friend has a nice office or meeting space, offer a fair price to use the space occasionally.

Do you need to talk to your board members between meetings?
Avoid hounding them but definitely call on them as resources when necessary. Many issues can be resolved via a quick email exchange. You may need to arrange short, impromptu meetings if a tough issue comes up.

Do board members have any rights in your company?
No! Remember, they are in place to help you grow, not to run your company or make ultimate decisions.

What a Board Provides

Of course before I created a board, I had no idea how much I needed one. I couldn't have been more wrong about that. My board brought me accountability, knowledge, and challenges that have pushed our company and me to new heights and a more stable future.

The accountability the board provides is crucial. I know the goals I set will be brought before me repeatedly. I also can rely on these three people to challenge my decision process. Without such a board, many business owners are left with few individuals to challenge them in any way.

How It Has Worked for Them: Michael Hosford

The use of a board of advisors at key points in our organization's development and my development as a leader has been invaluable. The positive impact that has occurred from taking time to prepare for the meetings, listening to seasoned executives and the follow-up conversations helped to shape the major decisions that have taken place over the past 30 years of running an ever-evolving technology service business. We would not be the company we are today without the wisdom gained from leveraging a board of advisors.

In addition, an unexpected outcome has been the discussions that have occurred related to my family and personal life. Success brings with it many opportunities and challenges and having good board of advisor members to help guide you through the many stages of business and personal triumphs and failures brings perspective and wisdom for the ride that you are on.

—*Michael Hosford*, Vartek Services Inc.

In addition to challenging me, my board of advisors help me see things in ways I never would have previously considered. They help me set realistic, achievable, important goals for my company and for myself. For instance, before I had a board, I did not quite understand how to use metrics.

I knew hard work pays off and that we were growing, but whenever anyone asked why or how, I had no specific answer. I could only shrug and tell them, *"Uh…we work harder to make things happen."* Today, I know that working harder only works so long. My board and I discovered together the key performance indicators we should measure. Some examples of such simple metrics include: net profit, key performance index, and closing percentage of first-time customers and maintenance agreement

(Comfort Family™) customers. As we started to understand where our growth came from, we were able to target market, and we became more proactive in producing and measuring metrics. At my board's urging for more metrics, we added a business analyst to our staff. Pending the urgency, for many years now, I've been provided with daily, weekly, and monthly metrics, which helps me make critical decisions. If a manager does not know in the first week of a new month that their department is behind on a goal, they can't make the necessary adjustments. These metrics might be part of a dashboard or in snapshot form, but whichever one you prefer, try to keep it simple. Without my board pressing me for those details, I might have never taken that vital step.

My board also prompted a dramatic change in our hiring procedures. I recall mentioning my difficulty in hiring service technicians. The human resources expert on my board called me out on that weakness. That discussion opened the door for an overhaul of our recruiting, interviewing, and decision-making processes. At the time I simply performed one or two relatively loose interviews before hiring. I personally tended to hire the applicants I had the most things in common with, but that seldom resulted in long-term employment. Now we have a list of specific questions conducted by various team members. Unless it's for a key position, I rarely interview nowadays. Not only has this made our hiring process more professional, it's a system that helps us hire and retain good people.

If I did not have a human resources expert on the board to help improve our processes, we would not have hired some of the talent we have today. We've also found people who fit our culture and are more likely to stay—*"people who stick"*, as we say today.

Other Ways to Be Teachable

Being teachable means you have the mindset of a lifelong learner. You must be consistently open to learning from anyone, at any time, on any topic. If you are a teachable leader, your company will excel beyond your own limits. On the other hand, a leader who is not teachable will hinder the company by his or her own stubbornness.

Everyone has blind spots. If you don't think you do, you may have more than average. To achieve success and fulfill your dream, you must realize you have faults, and you must be willing to allow someone to point them out to you in order to help you navigate through them.

Learning with a Coach

As valuable as a board can be, entrepreneurs may need a different kind of help in specific situations. While you can think of your board as experienced advisors, consider a business coach as a trainer who can target a specific part of your business.

If you are setting out to hit a particular goal, it can be a great benefit to hire a business coach who has already accomplished that specific task. An ideal candidate is someone in your industry who has grappled with similar challenges but has achieved more success than you have.

A business coach does not require a face-to-face meeting. I've been coaching for several years now, mostly by phone or video conferencing. Several business owners I've worked with over the phone have increased revenue by 300 percent and have put systems in place that allow them to sleep far better at night.

Allow me to be very clear on what a business coach is and is not: A business coach is *not* someone you hire to tell you what to do. Rather, a business coach *is* someone who asks you many questions, positively influences you, and helps pull from you the answers and results you need.

I must admit now that in my initial stages of coaching business owners, I did it wrong. Although I still sometimes share what has worked for us, as you have already read in the early parts of this book, this may not provide the results a client needs. I've learned to challenge others to come up with *their* own answers, the ones needed in *their* businesses and the ones that work with *their* culture.

One of my business coaches had an odd way of helping me to progress. He asked me to put deadlines on specific goals. He then asked me to write a check for an amount large enough that it would hurt if I were to lose it. He promised to send the check back to me if I met my goal by the deadline. However, if I didn't meet my goal, he would mail the check to the person I would least want to have it! That money, hanging in the balance, pushed me to work toward those goals. Thankfully, I accomplished what I set out to do, and I rescued my money from falling into undesirable hands. I challenge you to try a similar approach, but remember that it works only if you choose a dollar amount large enough to hurt.

You can get away with building your business on your own for a while. I did so for many years, but the concept of trying harder each year eventually caught up with me and I hit my capacity lid and was starting to burn out. Taking your business beyond your own capabilities first requires the humbleness to realize that you need help. A good friend of mine used to speak a solid truth: *"Be humble or you shall stumble."* Secondly, we must open up to the wisdom of others and be willing to learn from them. This takes time and will not happen overnight, but when you have a teachable spirit and are willing to implement what you learn, you will experience your dream coming closer and closer to reality.

Coaching Case Study

A business owner once called with an interest in my coaching program. He said his major problem was that he had been stuck at the $2 million mark for several years in a row and that his fifty-year-old family company, which used to be number one in his community, had dropped back a few places and he didn't know what to do about it. He was a third generation company, but the first and second generation still held the reigns.

He'd been pushing the first two generations hard for change but not having luck. He realized that the style of business has drastically changed since generation one ran things, but generation one was just not able to see that. The competition, which was coming on strong with better advertising and marketing, was now affecting revenue and profit margins.

After asking many questions, I helped him determine that he must have a "come to Jesus" meeting with the older generations. He realized that he could no longer run the business with his hands tied as they were. I suggested that if the older generations wanted to continue to attempt to run the business as they had, he might suggest to them that he step down and let them continue to run it all. I'm not quite sure if he said it as I did, but he made some progress and broke through a wall that had been there for many years.

Coaching is all about asking questions and challenging the client to think differently. Occasionally, I get a little firm and just directly ask, *"Why are you doing that again?"* or *"You've been doing that for a few years. Where has it got you?"* The famous Michael Jordan has quipped, *"A coach is someone that sees beyond your limits and guides you to greatness!"* If the greatest basketball player in the world needed a coach, I would say we all do.

When I started receiving emails and phone calls from HVAC business owners inquiring about common business issues, my experience and "school of hard knocks" education allowed me to ask them a few questions and help resolve their concerns.

"If you're looking to really improve your business and quality of life then Greg McAfee is the real deal. He saved our small, struggling HVAC business from going under, not to mention he saved the sanity of my family. It is always hard to trust people these days, especially when so many are only out to make a quick buck off you. Greg truly wants to help and has the experience and tools to really affect your business and your personal life. I can write on and on about the things I learned from Greg and cannot sincerely thank him enough for what he's done for me. Three years later we have doubled our annual sales, have a wonderful culture and environment where our staff enjoy coming to work every day, and have solved all operation and logistics issues. Now everything is running ridiculously smoothly, improved our image unbelievably, but most importantly I now love what I do again and my family is relaxed and happy too. If you're serious about moving to the next level in your business and as a person, then I wouldn't look any further. Stop suffering and call Greg before it's too late!"

"I have been working with Greg McAfee for the last six months and I have experienced very positive results.

With Greg's help, we just had our most profitable month EVER and we are on our way to set new records in annual revenue. We are up 40 percent from this time last year. He has helped us implement proven and effective business strategies. I highly recommend Greg McAfee to anyone looking to take that next step in building their business. We recently signed up for the 'Business Builder' program and are very excited! Thanks, Greg!"—Program Member

"Everyone needs a coach." —Bill Gates

2018 Greg McAfee HVAC Business Boot Camp.

CHAPTER THREE

Be a Leader

"I worry that business leaders are more interested in material gain than they are in having the patience to build up a strong organization, and a strong organization starts with caring for their people."—John Wooden

At Firestone, we had a supervisor we could easily describe as a classic micromanager. He enjoyed standing over us, watching as we worked. He often got in our way, and production increased only when he backed off. Once, just after unloading a truck full of tires in record time, Mr. Supervisor stood behind me, waiting for me to give him paperwork. He knew I looked forward to tallying up my count to make sure my count balanced, but he was rushing me to get to the next truck. Since I was an hour ahead of schedule, I told him to chill out and appreciate my swiftness or I'd convert to a slow speed (I should have told him how I really felt). He ended up walking away after realizing that I could slow down and cause him to stay over hours and that I would be finished ahead of time if he just left me alone.

From that experience, I learned that the best leaders give people the space they need to succeed, or fail, on their own. Instead of micromanaging, they step back and look at the entire field. They empower their team to work in their own way while still carrying out the overall values and mission. This equates to much better results.

In my own experience, I have learned that most leaders have a tendency to micromanage. When the buck stops with you and your name is on the door, it's hard to give up control. After all, we can do it better than anyone else, right? Well, not quite. Over time, I evolved from a boss into a leader.

Being a good leader means treating your team like team players rather than just employees. To do that, you must learn to appreciate your team members as valuable individuals with their own strengths, not just see them as bodies or employee numbers on the payroll system. You have to really get to know them as people in order to develop an understanding of what motivates them; in most cases, this goes far beyond their paychecks. You have to trust your people to do the jobs you used to do, even if they do them differently. Remember that *perfection can be the enemy of good*. You have to be flexible and humble enough to give them freedom to try new things, as well as to succeed and fail. Some may be born leaders, but we all have to develop our leadership skills. We do this by reading, taking leadership courses, benefiting from a leadership coach, and from experience itself.

How to Be a Better Leader

What kind of leader are you? A Florida business owner once complained to me that few of his more than eighty employees actually followed him. What kind of leadership is that? If you think you are a leader, turn around and see if anyone is following.

Good leaders have a few notable characteristics:

1. **Leaders are readers.** We can't all have lunch with people like John C. Maxwell, Dave Ramsey, or Jim Collins, but we can spend time pouring over their writings and thoughts

in their many books. Harry S. Truman remarked, *"Not all readers are leaders, but all leaders are readers."*

2. **Leaders are askers.** One of the most difficult challenges we face as leaders is to accept the fact that we may not know what is right or best in all situations. Most leaders ask questions because they are genuinely interested in learning the whys behind others' performance and decisions. Ed Broerman, God rest his soul, was a good friend and colleague who passed away at a very young age. Ed founded his HVAC company from scratch, and his techs drove all red trucks with yellow lettering. One day I asked Ed why he chose that color combination, and I still smile today when I recall his answer: *"When I went to buy my first work van, the car dealer had one left, and it was red, so I bought it, and the yellow lettering seemed to stand out."* Sometimes it's just that simple.

3. **Leaders are open-minded.** Having an open mind helps us think more critically, especially when we are faced with unpredictable circumstances. Keeping an open mind also helps us see the bigger picture when dreaming. Closed- or narrow-minded people are not leader material and should not hold leadership positions.

What is your leadership style? There are myriad of these, and many a book has been written on the subject to help business leaders identify their own styles and adapt the characteristics of successful leaders.

In the first edition of this book, I mentioned the Hersey and Blanchard Situational Leadership Model. That worked well, but today the Servant Leadership Model is a better tool that has assisted me in shaping and defining my path toward improving as a leader.

While the idea of servant leadership goes back two thousand years, Robert K. Greenleaf launched the modern servant leadership movement in 1970 with the publication of his classic essay, *"The Servant as Leader."* In that essay, he coined the terms *"servant-leader"* and *"servant leadership."* Greenleaf defined the servant-leader as follows:

"The servant-leader is servant first… It begins with the natural feeling that one wants to serve, to serve first. Then, conscious choice brings one to aspire to lead. That person is sharply different from one who is leader first, perhaps because of the need to assuage an unusual power drive or to acquire material possessions… The leader-first and the servant-first are two extreme types. Between them, there are shadings and blends that are part of the infinite variety of human nature… The difference manifests itself in the care taken by the servant-first to make sure that other people's highest priority needs are being served. The best test, and difficult to administer, is: Do those served grow as persons? Do they, while being served, become healthier, wiser, freer, more autonomous, more likely themselves to become servants? Moreover, what is the effect on the least privileged in society? Will they benefit or at least not be further deprived? The servant-leader is servant first." By that, he meant that the desire to serve, the *"servant's heart,"* is a fundamental characteristic of a servant-leader.

The master of servant leadership demonstrated this over two thousand years ago, and His example of servant leadership in historical texts is the example set out in Christianity as Jesus.

He embodied the idea that by serving others, you can empower them and help them see the way. He didn't perform His miracles for recognition or fame but to simply help people in need. The clearest examples of Jesus's model of servant leadership can be found in the Gospel of Mark:

Jesus called them together and said, "You know that the rulers in this world lord it over their people, and officials flaunt their authority over those under them. But among you, it will be different. Whoever wants to be a leader among you must be your servant, and whoever wants to be first among you must be the slave of everyone else. For even the Son of Man came not to be served but to serve others and to give His life as a ransom for many. Mark 10:42-45 (NIV)

Let's walk through some examples of how a servant leader portrays this in business. Those of you who practice servant leadership business will quickly recognize the following scenarios:

1. A team member's car breaks down. They have two kids in school and have to call Uber. You have three cars sitting in your parking lot or garage, not in use. Offer to let them borrow a car until theirs is repaired.

2. A team member's child is hospitalized, and the employee will miss a few weeks of work beyond paid time off. Slip some cash in an envelope with a note that says, *"Life throws us all curves at times, but I hope this helps until you get back to work."*

3. A new team member mentions that they attend church on Wednesday nights, but are on emergency call that night. Ask a few other technicians if they would be willing to switch on-call days to free up this team member on Wednesdays.

4. A supplier you spend thousands of dollars with monthly often takes you out to lunch. Occasionally, thank them by picking up the check and say, *"Thanks! Lunch is on me."*

There are many other examples of servant leadership. Jesus required it as a foundational character trait of anyone who followed Him, but He didn't just talk about it. He *was* it.

Every level of growth requires a higher level or skill of leadership. John Maxwell defines leadership as *influence*, nothing more and nothing less. Thus, as your company grows, your influence should increase. It just makes sense that the more you grow, the more you influence. If your influence does not increase, you may need to work to increase it.

How can you increase your influence? For starters, we improve our leadership skills by reading good books, taking leadership classes, and, for many like me, incorporating much prayer.

Like many young business owners, I portrayed some strong traits of rookie leadership. For many of my company's start-up years and then some, I made many mistakes and reacted incorrectly and too impatiently at times. Even though I learned a lot about leadership in the Marine Corps, I had much to learn about leading my own team, and I'm still learning even as I write this today. I found myself elbow deep in scheduling, marketing, running service, selling, and trying to manage appointments. In other words, I wore every hat. Slowly—very slowly—by hiring and training right, I managed to peel off those hats and pass those responsibilities over to someone else. Although some hats came off easy, please don't assume they all did. For me, the toughest to remove was sales. As the owner, I was sure I was the best salesperson and that no one could possibly outsell me!

Hiring Right

In order for me to take more hats off, I had to improve my hiring because it was a real obstacle at McAfee for many years. Do you have trouble finding the right people? So did we. Hiring the wrong person is a waste of time, energy, and resources and can affect morale. Today at McAfee, we've made many improvements in our processes. Even after we hire, we must be quick to notice when a team member is being inflexible or just doesn't fit in anymore. A manager should be close enough to the team to realize this and try to resolve the issue. If a bad attitude or disgruntlement has settled in so that the employee will not embrace change, we need to part ways sooner rather than later. A leader must be okay with moving people out, for both the good of the company and the good of the ill-fitting employee.

We have hired several salespeople who didn't work out for us, but we kept right on hiring until we found the right ones. We've hired and fired many people to find those who fit our culture, and have finally grasped the concept of hiring slow, firing fast!

An innovative person has to embrace problems and failure. Not everyone you hire will work out, not even with the best hiring practices in place. Many problems within my company, if not all, were caused by me. That said; guess who is responsible for all your problems? I take full responsibility for creating mine, fixing them, and doing all I can to keep them from happening again.

I recall being told that I'd never hit three million in revenue without hiring a professional salesperson. We all know what happens when we're told we can't do something. Not only did I hit that mark but I surpassed it. That said, I did my own selling for far too long. Looking back now, I practically burned out in my attempts to prove the naysayers wrong, and I actually caused us to lose business. My desire to excel at selling caused me to lose focus and take my eyes off the strategic target of my business. When you try to do everything yourself today, you don't have the time or energy to dream about where your company can be tomorrow.

I'd venture to say that many reading this book do not have businesses that operate smoothly. Instead, they may have created adult daycares. I know firsthand that it's a full-time job to run such a company. However, when we keep our focus on growing and managing, we can turn those adult daycares into actual for-profit businesses.

Because my main goal was to grow, I knew my leadership style had to change. I had to influence others in a positive, encouraging way and start serving them. "Do it because I'm the boss and I said so," was not working very well and caused a higher turnover rate.

Early on, I knew I didn't want to stay in the garage. One of my first trainees, Chris Bryant, left us to attend out-of-state training at a heating and air school. When he returned a year later, he inquired about being promoted from a helper to the position of service technician. I was hesitant at first, but Chris persuaded me to put him out in the field on his own so he could prove himself. I realized I was stifling the growth of my company, as well as his, because I refused to give him a chance. After much thought and his persuasion, I promoted Chris. He quickly became our go-to guy for troubleshooting. He surpassed my abilities multiple times. After learning this lesson, I became better at letting go. I realized it boils down to trust. Over the years, I've learned to trust more.

Most people want to excel, and as leaders, we have to recognize this and give them a chance to do so. Communication between Chris and me became two-way: I bounced ideas off him and vice versa. I'm glad to say that Chris is still with us today, serving as our very capable technical manager. He has trained many technicians along the way.

About six years into the business, I was still rotating myself in on emergency calls with my two technicians, a 24/7 chore.

Finally, after running calls all night, with much frustration and stress, I gathered my two technicians and told them I could no longer be on call. I shared with them that it was too difficult to run the business effectively while working all night.

In each of these circumstances, I took steps to both empower my workers and to free myself from the daily tasks of our business. The result was that I experienced more freedom to focus on the business. It freed me up to attend classes and conferences, which proved to be valuable learning opportunities. Because of that freedom, today I can share what I've learned with other HVAC leaders.

Do you feel you're too busy to attend conferences and/or seminars? Are you too consumed with putting out fires or just too stubborn to take the time to learn and grow? When you experience the freedom of letting go, you will improve your family time, as well as your own physical and mental health. One of the byproducts I experience in servant leadership is knowing that it is not all about me. The more I serve others, the better and stronger I become.

As a Christian, I often look to my Bible for guidance. There are endless versions and translations out there, but my favorite is my *Leadership Bible*. It helps me with most business and personnel issues I run into. On the topic of coaching, we can learn a lot from Moses and his father-in-law, Jethro. In Exodus 18, Jethro visits Moses and observes him settling disputes among the people of Israel. This never-ending, day-and-night conflict devours Moses's time and energy, so Jethro suggests an alternate plan:

The next day, Moses took his seat to serve as judge for the people, and they stood around him from morning till evening.

When his father-in-law saw all that Moses was doing for the people, he said, "What is this you are doing for the people? Why do you alone sit as judge, while all these people stand around you from morning till evening?"

Moses answered him, "Because the people come to me to seek God's will. Whenever they have a dispute, it is brought to me, and I decide between the parties and inform them of God's decrees and instructions."

Moses' father-in-law replied, "What you are doing is not good. You and these people who come to you will only wear yourselves out. The work is too heavy for you; you cannot handle it alone. Listen now to me, and I will give you some advice, and may God be with you. You must be the people's representative before God and bring their disputes to Him. Teach them His decrees and instructions and show them the way they are to live and how they are to behave.

"But select capable men from all the people, men who fear God, trustworthy men who hate dishonest gain, and appoint them as officials over thousands, hundreds, fifties, and tens. Have them serve as judges for the people at all times, but have them bring every difficult case to you; the simple cases, they can decide themselves. That will make your load lighter, because they will share it with you. If you do this and God so commands, you will be able to stand the strain, and all these people will go home satisfied."

Moses listened to his father-in-law and did everything he said. He chose capable men from all Israel and made them leaders of the people, officials over thousands, hundreds, fifties, and tens. They served as judges for the people at all times. The difficult cases, they brought to Moses, but the simple ones, they decided themselves. Exodus 18:12-25 (TLB)

What a great lesson in delegating and leadership! Listen to the wisdom in Verses 22 and 23: *"That will make your load lighter, because they will share it with you. If you do this and God so commands, you will be able to stand the strain, and all these people will go home satisfied."* Although delegation is not a new concept, it's not used as often as it should be. Moses listened to his father-in-law. We have a choice to make our load lighter, and when we make that choice, it will free us up to lead, train, and serve others.

Empowering Your Team

Like Moses, you must empower others to lead. If you don't give potential leaders on your team the freedom to lead, you will stifle their personal growth, as well as the growth of your business. This results in low morale, slow decision making, and fear. At McAfee, a select leadership team reports to me, the remaining team members report to them, and so on.

I've learned that hiring people who manage differently than I do creates a good mix, but we must have the same values and mission. Those who I train know the McAfee Way of doing business. Although their approach may be different, we all strive for and see similar results.

I discovered a longtime manager was no longer working by the guidelines of the McAfee Way. Unfortunately, I did not become aware of how disgruntled and dissatisfied he had become. It got so bad that he quit. Initially, it was a hard blow, but in time, I learned that his longtime bad attitude had affected many others; eventually, the atmosphere improved without him. However, I took full ownership of the incident. I shared with the leadership team that I had failed to keep my hand on the pulse; I should have noticed it earlier and possibly could have prevented the end result from being so devastating.

In the past, I held the reins much tighter. When I handed responsibilities over to my employees, I demanded that they call me every morning and evening with updates. That meant spending hours on the phone. Now, as things filter through my trusted chain of command, I receive the tough calls when necessary. This builds stronger teams, helps others grow, and decreases stress.

How It Has Worked for Them: Jim Bowman

As president of eighty-five-year-old industrial gas equipment company, Rexarc International Inc., Jim Bowman has learned the importance of training. "Think through and formulate a clear career path for the person you are looking to hire. Understand that they will only be 70 percent to 80 percent qualified for the position when you hire them but have a plan to develop them to the 100 percent level and then be sure you know where their next step will be in their career. Evaluate their capacity to help get there prior to hiring them. There are also professional testing agencies that will help you measure their capacity for growth."

Building a Culture by Training Your Team

At first it is very tough to allow others to make important decisions within your business. As the leader of a company, and especially if you are the founder, it is very easy to take the business personally. This is both good and bad. Eventually, you must let go. Of course there is risk involved when you empower others to make decisions and represent your company, but it's a risk that must be taken. One way to ensure success is to train people properly and continue to reiterate the core principles. In our company, that is the McAfee Way.

First, you must understand the culture you've created or have allowed others to create. That culture is a blend of values and beliefs developed over time. It's how you do business, and it is an integral part of building your brand, which we'll talk about in the next chapter. Building a culture and training within that culture go hand in hand. We begin explaining our McAfee Way as early as during the first job interview.

Because I lacked initial business training, I didn't realize until years later that I had actually established a very precise way of operating. Once this was discovered, we fine-tuned the strong principles and attempted to fade out the weak; we intentionally included the positive principles in all training. In fact, we launched a specific training group, McAfee University (MC-U), complete with t-shirts and training manuals that formally trained our team in the specific principles of our culture.

For years, others asked, *"What is the McAfee Way?"* and I could answer only with a list of what we did and how we did it. I couldn't specifically answer the question. When one of my advisors challenged me to put together a summary and keep it simple, I managed to narrow it down to a small card, shown on the next page.

INTEGRITY   CARE   CULTURE

The McAfee Way

Maintain **integrity** in all we do – both internally and externally.

Take **care** of people first – employees, customers and vendors – provide "WOW" service.

Demonstrate our **culture** which strives for perfection; performs things right the first time.

Give **consistency** to everyone – our customers, suppliers, and employees.

Be a growing and learning (**innovative**) organization; always ahead of competition.

Make wise decisions as a **team**, gather all information carefully; considering all options; implement decisions quickly. (Management to make decision when team cannot agree)

$$I \, C^3 \, IT$$

CONSISTENCY   INNOVATIVE   TEAM

MISSION STATEMENT
Leading in air quality, one home at a time.

VISION STATEMENT
To be recognized as an innovator and leader in the residential HVAC industry within the Miami Valley.

Just as athletic coaches train their teams through practice, so must we as business leaders. We do this in multiple ways. One of the most effective is role-playing.

Put your team in hypothetical situations to see how they react. We see great results from role-playing. Putting our team through these mock exercises reinforces the importance of developing people and soft skills that they will never forget. The results are positive and carry into homes and on phone calls with customers. We set up various scenarios, including greeting different types of homeowners (male, female, and couples). We even work on where to park our trucks at homes, when and where to put on shoe protectors, and how to work around pets, as all of these allow us to set the right tone and build rapport within the first few minutes of the appointment. We'd much rather fine-tune concerns in a mock setting than when we are live in front of a customer.

The sales team at McAfee, otherwise known as comfort advisors, learn to sell to various generations and demographics: single, married, elderly, and young families. Veteran staff members play the roles and pepper trainees with all the questions we hear daily on the job. In fact, we do our best to stump them. This method of training and sales presentation experience may seem intense, but it fully reinforces our particular values and expectations, further teaching everyone to follow the McAfee Way.

We put our customer service representatives through similar drills on the phone. We train and test on everything from voice tone to etiquette to politely taking control of the call. We believe so strongly in professional phone skills that we require an average of two weeks of training before we allow anyone to answer incoming calls, even just to place a customer on hold.

We believe in providing customers with a live operator to

help them, and we choose not to rely on automated answering, so we make sure each employee is trained in our specific method of greeting customers.

Intentional coaching helps our employees be more successful in their jobs because they are fully made aware of the parameters in which they are expected to work. We also prepare them by reminding them when busier than normal seasons are coming up, so they can prepare their families for less time at home.

You don't have to duplicate our culture to be successful, but you must determine what works best for your company and your customers and make sure your entire team sticks with it.

We invest in training throughout all seasons because we believe in the *kaizen* approach, a Japanese strategy for continuous improvement. Kaizen is more than a word; it's a mission—one that Toyota spearheaded as they shot to the top of the world of automobile makers. Some owners fear that thorough training entices employees to take their new skills to a competitor, but we fear the opposite: What if we don't train them properly and they stay with us? Besides, if they do happen to leave, which has occurred from time to time, at least we know they are trained correctly, and that helps raise the bar in our entire industry.

Another realm of training is helping the entire team understand the bigger picture. To accomplish this, we play a competitive board game I designed called TOBGOB: The Open Book Game of Business (www.tobgob.com). The intention is to help team members see and think like an owner. Four to five teams compete. They experience the reality of running a business. It's fun and challenging—a great way to foster a competitive spirit and help everyone better appreciate the many tough decisions required to effectively run a business.

Over time, the continual training of your staff on the

principles of your culture will transform your business and your leadership style. Start today by identifying the hallmarks of your culture so you can instill them in your people. Make a training plan, one that is as fun as it is challenging. You will all be better for it in the end.

Knowing Your Staff

We have already touched on this lightly, but it bears repeating: if you are going to be an effective leader, you must know your team. This should start during the interview process.

At McAfee, we ask applicants questions designed to reveal what is important to them. This might include inquiring about the books they've recently read or the amount of vacation they received at their last job and where they went on vacation. We give interviewees a stack of cards that contain our company values, such as integrity, honesty, and family. Then, we ask them to arrange the cards according to what is most important to them. They're instructed to narrow it down to five and, ultimately, two. Why? Because it is important for us to know what motivates the people who could potentially work at McAfee. At times, we even peek at their vehicles. Because we know that present behavior is an indicator of future behavior, if their cars are clean inside and out, we can safely assume they will keep our trucks, offices, and equipment clean and well maintained.

A few years ago, in an effort to learn a little more about our people, we asked our team members to complete a survey and list what they need from their company. Job security topped that list. Knowing this has taught us how to better work with our team.

That simple survey prevented us from trying to lead them blindly.

Knowing Your Style

As important as it is to know your team, it's also crucial to know yourself. Have you ever thought of asking your staff or leadership team to evaluate your leadership style and how it impacts them and the business? Do they see you the way you see yourself? When I asked my leadership team to tell me how they perceive my leadership style, I received the following valuable feedback:

From Chris B., Technical Manager, twenty-five years

How does Greg's leadership style play out for you in working with him?

"One of the strengths I see in Greg is his ability to see the vision for the future of the company. He has a natural sense of where we are going as a team and can easily break that vision up into what needs to be done to get there. Greg acts quickly and is capable of setting a plan in place in an instant. Once the plan is made, he is laser focused and does not deviate from the course.

While these are all great qualities, what really sets him apart is his communication of the plan to those around him. He holds regular meetings with his leadership team, his managers, each department, and the company as a whole. It's extremely important to him that we are all on the same page.

Another characteristic of Greg's leadership style is his tough-but-fair attitude.

It's not always an easy place to work; it is, however, extremely rewarding to know that you have pushed yourself to be your best each and every day. Greg will tell you when you've done something wrong. He definitely does not shy away from correcting your mistakes, but his goal is simply that you learn from it. I've found, in my career here, that it's best to own up to your mistake, explain what you'll do differently the next time, and move on. Greg never holds a grudge when a mistake has been made, but rather he uses it as a teaching moment."

How does that help you in coaching your own team?

"Greg expects me to perform at my best, and, in turn, that is what I expect from my team.

I manage many different employees at varying skill levels and with different strengths and weaknesses, but I expect the best from each and every one. Not only do I hold them accountable, but as a team, they hold each other accountable. We have a collaborative environment in which they are free to call on each other for help. There is no ego or pride in having to seek out assistance. Greg has shown that one thing to me. If he does not know the answer, he calls someone who does. We try to practice that in the field every day.

I also try to share the vision of the company's future with my team, just as Greg does with me. It's important that everyone knows where we are headed so our processes and procedures make sense. They must know the desired end result, as they play an integral part in the company getting there."

How has McAfee differed from other places you have worked?

"McAfee thrives on structure, which is different from most places. There are processes and procedures for everything we do, as well as a reason those processes and procedures are in place. When you know the why behind a process, you buy into that way of doing it. You don't have rules just for rules' sake; the rules must make sense to your team.

McAfee is all about being a team. We are all just one piece of the puzzle, and we rely on each other's strengths to complement our weaknesses. We are in this for the long haul, not just here to earn a paycheck (well, most of us).

The opportunities provided to McAfee employees go beyond the heating and air conditioning world. We are encouraged to develop as people and, many times, messages shared by Greg during meetings are applicable outside of work. Greg truly cares about each one of us and our families, just as he is passionate about supporting children and families in our community."

From Angie D., Director of Marketing, eighteen-years

How does Greg's leadership style play out for you in working with him?

"The leadership team is empowered by Greg to make decisions. Right or wrong, a decision is made. When wrong, we learn from our mistake and move on. The responsibility that comes with making decisions helps us grow as leaders. It also allows us to build on the knowledge needed to lead day-to-day operations, allowing Greg to work more on the company and not so much in the company. We are sought out regularly for our opinions and are involved in the strategic planning of the business. This reinforces the sense of team and reaffirms the value each one of us brings to the table. There are no lone rangers here; everything we do is a team effort.

Having worked with Greg for eighteen years, I can certainly see how the leadership style Greg had with me evolved over time. In the beginning, the leadership was more direct: "This is what you do… This is how you do it…

Don't do it that way… That is the wrong way to do it." I was micromanaged, but I admittedly needed it at the time. As I evolved in my understanding of McAfee, Greg's style of leadership evolved right along with me. I was encouraged to make decisions, but more importantly, I was encouraged to make a mistake."

How has McAfee differed from other places you have worked?

"The culture here is everything. We know who we are, what we do, and where we're going. We choose not to do things the way many other companies do. We're unique. When anyone new comes in, it takes a while to learn and embrace the McAfee Way of doing business. We are very well structured and organized, and expectations are high. We take it for granted that people are going to be on time and ready to work when they get here.

I know there are other companies out there having trouble just getting their employees to show up in the morning. Here, we don't have those kinds of problems because it's an expectation that we learn at time of hire. Everyone knows that is the McAfee Way and we adapt to it.

Several years back, I left McAfee for about a year to work for another company. My new employer did not share the same sense of urgency, the culture, or the guiding principles I had grown accustomed to. There was no direction, no course. Honestly, before I left McAfee, I wondered, Are those things really that important? I can tell you now that the answer is a resounding yes! They are that important, and everything matters!

In my absence, I developed a completely new appreciation for McAfee and its operations. I realized that those were not just McAfee principles anymore; they had become my own. Once this realization was made, I knew I simply could not work for any other company.

From Candice S., Accounting Manager/ Business Analyst, eleven years

How does Greg's leadership style play out for you in working with him?

Greg's leadership style encourages an autonomous working environment. As the accounting manager, I have the freedom to make decisions within my scope of expertise concerning my team with little interference from Greg. Trust is key. Greg doesn't stand over my shoulder each day, making sure I'm getting my job done and getting it done right. He has placed me in this role because of the trust he has in my ability. There is no micromanaging going on; rather, there are open lines of communication, and I am able to decide what works best for my team and then share those plans with Greg.

Greg sets the bar high for himself, his company, and his team. It is not always easy to accomplish the goals we set for the company and ourselves, but even when we miss the end target, we accomplish some amazing things along the way. Personally, his push to be the best keeps me motivated. While much of what we do in accounting is repetitive and may seem mundane, there are always new and exciting opportunities for growth. Greg is open to new processes, new reports, and new ways of thinking.

We are all encouraged to come up with new ideas, no matter how crazy they seem. We have frequent brainstorming meetings in which we can openly throw out suggestions. In these sessions, there are no bad ideas. Everyone remains open and positive, which makes for an extremely productive collaboration.

How does that help you in coaching your own team?

In managing my own team, I try to encourage independence. Once fully trained, I expect my team to take their job duties and run with them. I rarely check in on the status of a particular task, but I do ask my team at multiple points during the day if any issues have come up or if there is anything they need my help on. We have deadlines for our responsibilities; as long as those deadlines are met with an accurate result, there is no need for me to micromanage.

I feel like Greg takes this same approach in what I accomplish. He asks me every day if there is anything I need from him, and while the answer is usually no, his question keeps an open line of communication.

I also remain open to suggestions from my team, just as Greg is open to mine. While I know what has worked for us in the past, someone on my team may come up with a better way. It's important to hear out each and every suggestion. Not all will be implemented, but showing your team that their thoughts are important ensures that they will continue thinking of ways to improve and that they are completely comfortable sharing those ideas with you.

How has McAfee differed from other places you have worked?

Fortunately, I have been part of the McAfee team for eleven years, so my work experience is limited in comparison to most. Rather than address how it differs, let me explain reasons why I stay. I started with McAfee eleven years ago in a part-time position, assisting with filing and administrative duties. I enrolled in college, studying veterinary medicine—just about the farthest thing from heating and air. At that point McAfee was just a job for me. Not too long after I started, there was an opportunity to join the Customer Service Department in a full-time role.

I jumped at the chance, not really knowing where that position would take me. From Customer Service, I moved to Accounting as an assistant. After some time, I became an accounting manager. Somewhere during those transitions, I realized this is more than just a job. I have a career here! What other company would take a part-time administrative assistant through the ranks into a management role?

Of course, I changed to a business major and was able to earn both a bachelor's and master's degree while working at McAfee. This company has become more than just a job and more than a career. We are truly a family. I have worked with many of the same faces for a decade now. We've been together for many life milestones, both professionally and personally. Not only have we grown to love each other, but we also love each other's families. We celebrate successes in business but also successes in life. McAfee is truly our home away from home.

From Michael G., Comfort Advisor/Sales Manager, three years

How does Greg's leadership style play out for you in working with him?

"In my time working with Greg, I have come to find out what he is passionate about: everything! Of course, there are a few things he holds above all else: serving people, serving God, and working hard. Greg is the first person in the office each day and typically one of the last to leave. When he tells us, "I would never make you do something I wouldn't do myself," he means it. John Maxwell describes leadership as influence,

nothing more nothing less. Greg's influential reach has spread through his employees, his customers, and all over the country through his Greg McAfee Business Builder program. After countless meetings, a few one-on-ones, and the occasional, "Hey, Michael, you messed up," Greg has shown me what true leadership looks like, and he pushes each member on his team toward success."

How does that help you in coaching your own team?

I have learned from Greg to lead by example. I would never ask anyone I work with to do something I would not do myself. Greg has also taught me that there is a time for motivating a team and there are times to discipline a team. You have to take the positives in step with the negative. He has also shown me the importance of being in tune with the people who are working for you. If something seems off with someone, go out of your way to make sure they are well taken care of. This goes extremely far.

How has McAfee differed from other places you have worked?

Being young in my professional career, I can't say too much about how McAfee differs from prior employers. What I can say is that the culture at McAfee would be difficult to replicate. We are all working together, and when one member or department needs help, we all pitch in. Very few people enjoy coming in to work every day, but McAfee has created that. It's not because of the business we are in, but because we are all driven to serve others, both the people we work with and the customers we serve.

I am proud to tell people I work for McAfee Heating and Air.

2019 McAfee Headquarters (30,000 square feet).

CHAPTER FOUR

Be Well Known

"Your brand is all about your values. It's who you are, it's what you do and it must be what you stand for." —Greg McAfee

When I started McAfee Heating and Air, I was an unknown tech in a truck. I had not lived in the area very long. I did not have family from here and definitely did not have a household name. I knew it was going to take hard work and whole lot of hustle to create a name for myself in business. My vision was to operate a well-known company. Anyone who is going to risk starting their own business must be willing to make sure everyone knows who they are and why they are the best choice. It was not a desire rooted in ego; rather, it stemmed from a competitive streak that drives me not only to win, but also to dominate—with passion—all endeavors. That drive has served me very well in the world of marketing, and twenty-five years later, we rose from number 486 to number 1 in our residential HVAC market, now having a very recognizable name.

It's simple: if someone is going to use your service, they have to know your name. However, getting them to remember you is not as simple. You need to figure out who your market is, meaning whom you want to serve, and then get your name in front of them as often as possible.

In the seven years since completing the first version of this book, much has changed. With Facebook and other social media platforms, targeting and reaching specific customers is much easier. I hope you have considered whom you want to reach. Is it the homeowner, property owner, or commercial building manager? At McAfee, we focus most all our effort on reaching homeowners. Specific age groups, income levels, and home prices determine how we market to them.

Often in my coaching sessions, I ask about targeted customers. The answers vary: *"People with money,"* or *"I don't know."* These vague answers will not serve a business well. The question of target marketing needs answered prior to even considering the avenue of advertising.

The options for advertising and getting your name out there are endless today and can be overwhelming at first. Nevertheless, as you design the right strategy to reach existing clients and the potential clients you prefer, your phone will begin to ring.

Advertising is a risk of its own. However, it should be thought of as an investment. If you know who your market is and when and where to market to them, it can pay big dividends. On the other hand, if you squander your hard-earned money randomly on just any media, in any time slots, you will lose what you've invested. From the get-go, you have to accept that even your best efforts may not work as quick as you'd like.

One risk factor for those in HVAC is that we are a very weather-driven field. We could spend $20,000 on an advertising campaign, but a sudden, significant change in our sporadic Ohio weather could result in either a homerun or a strikeout, with little to no immediate return. We take that risk when we invest in advertising.

One major mistake small businesses make is looking at

advertising as an expense they cannot afford rather than a necessary calculated risk. It can take decades to build a strong word-of-mouth business. In fact, it took us ten to fifteen years to build a consistent stream of business from referrals. It's a wonderful compliment when a customer calls and tells us they've heard great things about us from a trusted friend. However, relying on word-of-mouth alone will make your business growth an even slower, more arduous process.

As trite as it is, the old adage is true: You really do have to spend money to make money. Annually, we budget 6 to 9 percent of our gross revenue for advertising and marketing. As we've grown, our advertising dollars have increased, but the percentage remains the same. I encourage you to set a percent of your annual budget for annual marketing and stick with it.

How It Has Worked for Them: Louis Hobaica

Louis Hobaica, president of Hobaica Services Inc., in Phoenix, Arizona, sees advertising not as an expense, but as a necessity. "Advertising is essential for a thriving and successful business. Whether you spend your marketing budget with your employees or with outside sources, it is essential. Marketing is like watering a plant: Water it properly, and it will thrive. Provide little or no water, and it will wither away and die! Downtimes are when you need to increase your marketing efforts, as most of your competition will slack off, and you will have much better results and exposure. For any maintenance/repair/retrofit company, I recommend budgeting at least 5 percent of total sales for marketing."

How to Kill Your Business in Ten Easy Steps

1. **Don't advertise.** Just pretend everyone already knows what you have to offer.
2. **Don't advertise.** Tell yourself you don't have time to spend thinking about your business.
3. **Don't advertise.** Just assume everyone already knows what you sell.
4. **Don't Advertise.** Convince yourself that you've been in business so long that customers will automatically come to you.
5. **Don't advertise.** Forget that there are new potential customers who might do business with you if they were invited to do so.
6. **Don't advertise.** Forget that you have competition who is trying to attract your customers away from you.
7. **Don't advertise.** Tell yourself it costs too much and that you don't get enough out of it.
8. **Don't advertise.** Overlook the fact that advertising is an investment in selling and not an expense.
9. **Don't advertise.** Be sure not to provide an adequate advertising budget for your business.
10. **Don't advertise.** Forget that you have to keep reminding your established customers that you appreciate their business.

What's the bottom line? If you want to avoid killing your business, you have to **ADVERTISE!**

We started small by advertising in a local direct-mail magazine and the phone book, sponsoring a Little League team, and plastering my truck with our company name. Today, we show up on television, radio, a variety of digital and social media, and several Little League, basketball teams and even on race cars. Over the years we have invested in building a brand and a successful advertising strategy. This may sound peculiar, but we didn't intentionally start out building a brand; as mentioned,

I didn't have any training in marketing, advertising, or branding prior to starting my business. Fortunately, I have learned through reading and specific classes, and I pray for wisdom and insight.

Marketing, Advertising, and Branding

These terms are often used interchangeably, but they are actually three distinct concepts that tend to overlap. To make the most out of your investment, it is worth studying the differences.

Marketing

Marketing is the process of attracting then interesting potential customers/clients in your products and/or services. The key word in this marketing definition is *process*, as marketing involves researching, promoting, and selling to your customer. What does that mean to an entrepreneur? Imagine marketing as the overall strategy for reaching your customers. A marketing plan includes all the aspects of promotion, such as advertising, public relations, brand identity, sales strategy, social media, customer service, and community involvement. These all work in unison to market your services or products and build the type of reputation you want to be known for.

Advertising

One of the most important pieces of your marketing puzzle is advertising.

Paid for, and controlled by, the company, advertisements focus on building brand awareness and driving sales. Ads can be delivered digitally or via mail, or appear on radio, television, or in print. Knowing the demographics of your target customer is critical in figuring out the best medium for advertisement.

Advertisements must work independently while also being integrated with the other components of your marketing plan. Too many HVAC companies mistakenly think running a TV commercial or radio spot or publishing a Facebook page is all it takes. They are left disappointed when a rush of business does not follow. Advertising can be a powerful tool, but it does not work in a vacuum. It must remain relevant and active.

Branding

Branding is very important: it is your company's promise to the customer. Entrepreneur.com defines it this way: *"[Branding] tells them what they can expect from your products and services, and it differentiates your offering from that of your competitors. Your brand is derived from who you are, what you stand for, and what people think you stand for."*

A branding strategy lays out who you are and what your values are. It should mirror the brand your customers see, feel, and touch. Your brand strength should be measured in years and decades, and not just days and months. Consistency is vital to the success of your brand.

You need the same look and message to be evident inside and outside your company. One part of that look is your name. Your business name is like a handshake, as it says a lot about you and makes a first impression. Next is your logo, often the most visual connection anyone has with a product or company before, during, and after a business relationship. The style and color should contribute to a professional image.

Backing It Up with Brand Identity

You may spend a high percentage of revenue on advertising and still suffer failure in your business if your company does not live up to its promises. Your standards for customer service and work quality must match the image you portray. If we had failed to staff our company adequately to pull off that new work schedule, we wouldn't have been able to handle it when the calls started pouring in. If our customer service representatives and service technicians were not well trained in our brand identity, our actions would counteract the professional image of trust we portray in our ads.

Be consistent in your marketing and advertising. Your company colors, logo, and slogan should be the same across every platform so they will become recognizable over time. We all know that Coca-Cola font, the apple with a bite out of it, and that swoosh on a pair of athletic shoes. Branding gives a company a chance to differentiate themselves from the rest and set the image it wants to impart. It is paramount that you realize it can take years, even decades, to build a brand.

Examples of Great Brands

Several companies have built gold-standard brands with their customer service and consistency. The $10 billion fast-food restaurant chain Chick-fil-A has built its brand on its values, setting it apart from its competitors and leading to rapid, consistent growth. Founder S. Truett Cathy built the chain on biblical principles, paying close attention to customer service. Although he has passed away, his son Dan has taken hold of the reins and runs the company with the same fervent passion as his father. Workers often circulate the restaurant floor to tend to customer needs, and at the end of every transaction, they say, *"It's my pleasure."* More importantly, they say it as if they mean it! Notably and commendably, Chick-fil-A is the only fast food chain that chooses to close on Sundays. Among his top ten tips for entrepreneurial success, Cathy says, *"Be kind to people. Courtesy is very cheap but brings great dividends."* Today, Chick-fil-A is a clear example of branding being more than just a logo or marketing campaign. Today they're experiencing fifty-one years of growth, make more revenue than several fast food competitors combined, and are still closed on Sundays.

The Walt Disney Company has established a ubiquitous brand. According to the Disney Institute, an arm of the company that teaches its principles, Disney credits its success to the powerful link between guest satisfaction and brand reputation. Disney trains its employees to create *"magical moments"* that keep guests coming back. *"If we focused on those kinds of moments, could we maintain them on a daily basis? Absolutely not!"* Disney Institute Facilitator Nicole Lauria said. *"We must do these little things too. Never underestimate the power of what seems like small initiatives."* Remember that if you can improve the little things, the big things normally take care of themselves.

You must determine and know what you stand for and be so passionate about it that people just enjoy doing business with you.

What is Effective?

If your business is new or you have not thought about these concepts before, it can be a lot to take in. Long gone are the days of just placing an ad in the local penny saver or on the radio and waiting for your phones to start ringing. The leading businesses today are savvy marketers who have built well-known, solid brands. They take advantage of many tools to reach their customers. What works best? Where should you invest? You need to know the answers to these questions.

The more you study the demographics and understand where

your growth comes from or should come from, the better you'll know where and how to market as well as where to advertise. I've tried marketing techniques or venues for six to twelve months to determine how effective or ineffective they were. If you don't see any return on your investment after a year, it's obviously not a good place to spend your advertising dollars.

We even gathered a focus group of six to ten customers to examine our ads before going live. We asked what they liked and disliked about the ads. That tactic was remarkably informative and saved us money.

Ask yourself three questions: *Are we targeting the right audience? Is what we're advertising airing enough to resonate with potential customers? Do we come across as who we really are?* For us, the right combination of advertising has been television, radio, and, most recently, digital and social media.

Market Research

We have also invested in much research to find out more about our target market. Why? Because we can't sell them what they need or want if we don't know who they are and what they need or want. In today's world, we can follow our customers' shopping patterns online through search engine optimization, and we have the option to post paid advertisements where they shop. I am aware that by the time you read this book, some new technology will likely be available.

The Face of the Company

I used to appear in all our commercials as the face of the company. Now I'm still sprinkled throughout them, mostly in the form of my voice. Rarely do local business owners appear in their own commercials. Some national brands use their leaders, such as George Foreman with his grill. Many people do not realize there was a real Colonel Sanders who founded Kentucky Fried Chicken. Although he passed away in 1980, his is the iconic face that still decorates their *"finger-lickin' good"* boxes and buckets.

If something happens to the face of the company (such as death or embarrassing incidents), the company's brand could be affected instantly. This is why, over the past few years, we have gradually transitioned me from the main screen. That plan has been very successful. It's not always best that a business owner appear in his or her company advertisements. If you are uncomfortable on camera or the message does not produce results, you should search for alternative talent.

Hiring a Marketing Firm

Does it help to hire a marketing firm? Maybe, but you need to be ready for that. Unfortunately, some small business owners hire big advertising firms they can't afford or they hire companies that have little or no experience helping mom-and-pop shops sprout into something bigger.

Smaller marketing firms or individuals who have the right experience can be a great asset to your company's marketing plan. Make sure the company or person you choose has previous experience with your business, as we know not all marketing firms will have the same expertise. In addition, seasonal businesses must be handled with a special touch.

You can also consider hiring a business coach, like me, who has a history and success in the kind of business you are in— someone who can help you strategize your marketing before you ever need an agency.

Entering Contests

We've won accolades such as the BBB Eclipse Integrity Award; BBB Torch Award; The HVACR News Best Contractor to Work for Award, our first national award; multiple *Dayton Business Journal* Best Places to Work Awards; and, as I write, we were honored to be inducted into the Dayton Business Hall of Fame. These recognitions earned us local and national publicity that continue to separate us from the competition. It can also be a nice boost for your team when you win.

To the hundreds of business owners, and companies I have worked with, I suggest entering contests. It's a great honor to be nominated for an award by an employee or customer. It is also a strong marketing move. It places positive information about your company in the consumer's eye.

How Winning Awards Have Helped This Company: Theo Etzel

At Conditioned Air, we've been fortunate to receive recognition as a company at the national and local levels as well as individual recognitions for team members. There is a major distinction between third party awards and honors and being the recipient of a manufacturer award. Manufacturer awards, while nice, are usually based on purchase amounts reaching certain levels. The quality of the company and ethics involved are not typically weighted too heavily. The consumer is smart enough to know the difference between sales awards and behavioral based honors.

Over the years we've received the ACCA National Residential Contractor Award as well as a local Uncommon Friends Foundation Business Ethics Award. Our former CFO and partner received the Outstanding Woman in HVAC. We've been recognized on an industry wide basis and in our hometown as a Best Places to Work business. For each of these awards we produced a PR piece through our PR company and usually got a follow-up article in various publications as well as TV coverage. This does several things: The team gets a big pride boost in the company; the good will generated in the marketplace is excellent; and it allows people to talk about credibility and what separates us from others, not by putting them down (never do that) but elevating our ethics and behaviors. We use the award logos in our advertising as well.

One word of caution: if you haven't been behaving, as a company, to the criteria of the recognition you wish to apply for, don't apply. Change your corporate culture and actions before submitting to the scrutiny of the application. Remember, if you win awards under false pretenses and don't honestly and sincerely behave like an award-winning team, then your credibility goes out the window. The team members see right through this because the leadership can't be trusted, and they see right through the falsehood. And, with the advent of social media, it won't be long before consumers will be writing about how you're not living up to the "award winning" expectations that have been set in the marketplace. If you're not going to live it, don't list it.

—*Theo Etzel*, Conditioned Air Company, LLC.,
Chairman of the Board

CHAPTER FIVE

Be Giving

"Make all you can. Save all you can. Give all you can."
—John Wesley

One of the most moving experiences in my life as a business owner came through a random opportunity to give to a family in need. It was close to Christmas, and my wife heard about a local woman who was taking in four children from an abusive situation in a neighboring state. When Naomi told me the heart-wrenching story, I knew we had to do something to help. The children had experienced every type of abuse imaginable, as well as things no one would ever want to imagine.

We presented the story to our team, and without hesitation, everyone rallied to help. Through the generosity of our team, the foster mom was able to provide new clothes, supplies, and toys for the kids that Christmas. That sweet woman shared with us:

I had the pleasure of working with Mr. McAfee through his generous Children's and Youth Program. He helped orchestrate an outreach plan for four new foster children. Greg put his idea into action and continues to do so for other children through the McAfee Foundation. He is not only touching the lives of children he has never met but also really changing sorrowful situations for many children who would be at a disadvantage otherwise.

I do not mention this to boast. In actuality, what we provided for that family was minor compared to the overall needs of the children, and the parents who ended up adopting them should get all the kudos. Nevertheless, it was a special experience because we quickly mobilized for something more important than the daily grind of business. We pulled together as a team and responded because we felt called to do so. When you build a team that cares about people and a business that has the resources to give, you can experience the joy of giving to others in crisis.

Philanthropy Is Good for Business

Each Christmas, the law firm of Minor & Brown in Denver, Colorado, gives each employee twenty one-dollar bills. The workers then fan out across the city, finding organizations and people who can use the money to make a difference, even a small one.

Similarly, and on a bit larger scale, Target Corporation gives out $500 million a year to support education and literacy nationwide. Their CEO proudly says the company has always believed in strengthening the communities in which it does business.

Philanthropy may be a big word, but even the smallest businesses can and should participate in it. From the local mom-and-pops to giant corporations, companies are the driving force behind much of the philanthropy in this country. In fact, the great majority find some way to give. According to the Better Business Bureau, 91 percent of small businesses give to charity, and 83 percent give through volunteering their time. Perhaps some give only for tax breaks and/or to generate good publicity; however, for many entrepreneurs, the thrill of success really comes from being able to use their resources for something greater than themselves.

I try to ingrain a giving spirit throughout McAfee Heating and Air. We approach philanthropy in a variety of ways. We see it as an opportunity to pay it forward—not so much giving back, because that would imply that we'd taken something in the first place. Our desire to help is manifested in our selfless attitude towards how we approach every job, in giving financially to organizations and individuals through our foundation (which I'll explain later), and in the way we share our time to help others.

We have been in the giving mode since we first opened our doors. My wife and I sponsored a Little League team the first year in business and we enjoyed going to their games! When the season ended, we took the team out for ice cream. It was a simple gesture, but it was an important start in what would become a principle of business that I believe has helped carry us to this level of success.

When I help others, it makes it about much more than just me. Although revenue is important and we couldn't help others without profits, that's not what the major focus is. It is about whom we can help along the way. We are laser focused on our responsibility to help meet the needs of those around us, children in particular. A question we ask frequently is, *"How can we help someone experience something they couldn't otherwise experience on their own?"*

Creating a Culture of Selflessness

Most people assume giving starts with a check written to a charity or by putting in a few hours of volunteer time. From a business standpoint, though, it really starts with the standards you set for how you treat your employees and customers. Giving should start with you as in the way you pay your people and provide employment benefits. I've extended no-interest loans to employees caught in tough situations, allowing them to pay us back over time. Why? Because when my employees are able to build solid lives for their families, it helps me carry on with my dream, and the dreams of my employees can be interwoven with their work at my company.

A selfless culture also extends into the homes we service. We spend thousands of dollars each year on shoe protectors. Why? It's certainly not because it's a good policy or impressive, and they don't really make a fashion statement. It's because we truly care about the homes we step foot in. We want to respect the customers who are gracious enough to give us their business. Because we value our customers' time and schedule, we call ahead, and we honor their time by being prompt. If we happen to underestimate a price quote, that mistake is on us, and we don't hold our customer accountable. We don't say anything about it; we just honor our original estimate and do the job, despite the loss.

It will be difficult to engage your employees in meaningful charity work if they feel the company doesn't respect them or your customers. When you set a high standard of caring, your team members are more likely to share your enthusiasm for helping others. I am hopeful that even if I were not here, McAfee Heating and Air would still be a giving company because of the standards we've ingrained into our culture.

Being Generous

I find giving to be fulfilling and rewarding. Not that I give with the expectation of getting something in return, because it's not about that. I do experience the blessing of giving though, because it seems to come back many times over in some form.

While I believe philanthropy is a corporate responsibility, telling other entrepreneurs to give away precious profits because it is the right thing to do can be a hard sell. Let's take a look at the business case for giving. A recent report from the Committee for Encouraging Corporate Philanthropy gives insight into research-backed reasons for corporate giving.

Company giving enhances employee engagement. Employees are more motivated and loyal to a company when they feel engaged through group volunteer programs and know about their company's philanthropy. It provides a sense of identification with the organization.

Company giving builds customer loyalty. According to the report, a company's commitment to communities and certain philanthropic causes enhanced brand perception, customer loyalty, repeat business, and word-of-mouth promotion.

Company giving contributes to business innovation and growth opportunities. Philanthropy also gives businesses new relationships and opportunities to test and demonstrate new ideas, technologies, and products.

A study conducted by Deloitte LLP highlights another benefit: stronger recruitment. A company's philanthropic initiatives can set it apart for a job candidate. Deloitte researchers found that 72 percent of employed Americans deciding between jobs in which all other factors were the same (location, job description, pay, and benefits) said they would choose the company that also supports charitable causes.

Giving Financially: Make a Plan

It's important, even as a small business, to manage your giving professionally. Philanthropy can be part of your strategic planning. During planning, consider some important questions that will help guide your giving:

- What kinds of causes do we feel most passionately about? Which ones align with our business?
- How much should we give of our profits annually? On average, small businesses give 6 percent of net profits annually to charity, according to an American Express study.
- Should we give through a foundation? Should we manage the foundation ourselves or use an outside firm such as an accountant, attorney, or community foundation that offers services for donor-directed funds?
- How will we research the individuals and organizations that request help?
- Will we seek or accept publicity for our donations?
- How will we communicate with our employees about our giving? Will we discuss it in meetings and in-company newsletters?
- Will employees be asked to give? How?
- Will we participate in community fundraising campaigns such as the Red Cross or the Salvation Army?

Reviewing these points can help make giving a joyful experience instead of a burden. It will set a framework for giving that can grow with your company.

How It Has Worked for Them: Jim Bowman

Jim Bowman, chief executive officer of Rexarc International Inc., says his company makes sure the values of the charitable organization dovetail with its corporate values. "Be proactive and target a few charitable organizations in advance and at the annual budgeting process for the next fiscal year rather than just using the first-come, first-served approach and making a knee-jerk promise at an emotional point to a phone solicitation," he said.

Why We Started a Foundation

As mentioned, we've given to a variety of organizations. Part of our strategic planning included giving to a local organization that aligned with our mission of improving air quality and helping youth. After several years in business, we initiated The McAfee Foundation for Children and Youth to focus our giving on children and youth with pulmonary issues. This made our processes more professional and gave us a formal way to solicit donations from our employees (through a payroll deduction), as well as from our customers, who were offered a chance to give one hundred dollars to the foundation in return for purchasing a high-efficiency air cleaner.

The foundation supports individuals, as well as groups.

A few years ago, in our desire to support a local organization dedicated to children and clean indoor air, we began a partnership with the Children's Pulmonary Department. The hospital uses our donations to purchase supplies such as inhalers, to help parents with the cost of gas to get to and from the hospital, and to cover insurance co-pays for families who are struggling to afford medical care for their children. The hospital also refers families to us who need a cleaner indoor air environment for their children who suffer from ailments like lung cancer or severe allergies. We have donated air duct cleanings and high-efficiency air purification systems, repaired and replaced heating and cooling systems, and added special filters. About 80 percent of proceeds go to Dayton Children's Hospital.

Donating Time

Even when economic times are tough, you don't have to back-burner your giving. If your ability to donate financially declines, I challenge you to be creative in your philanthropy. There's no reason it can't continue by different means. In fact, it could be a great elixir for low morale during difficult times. Often, the magnitude of your own problems shrinks in light of the hardships others are facing. Viktor E. Frankl, Holocaust survivor and author of the 1946 book *Man's Search for Meaning*, shared that the concentration camp survivors who tried to give purpose to their days by helping others were more likely to survive.

We've found several ways to give in addition to financial donations. For instance:

- Our team once collected old cell phones for an organization that distributes them to domestic abuse survivors who use them during emergencies. Some nonprofits need your time and expertise as much as they need monetary donations.

- Consider sitting on the board of a nonprofit you're interested in. You will meet new people and help the organization.
- Can you tutor or serve as a special speaker at a school? Look for community-wide days of service to find easy opportunities to plug in and make a difference.

Dreaming Beyond Yourself

Some people think a business should grow and prosper first and give back later. I believe the opposite is true: I grow and give simultaneously. If you make giving part of your culture from the very beginning, it will be easier to continue giving along the way.

I challenge you, wherever you are financially, to find a way for your business to impact the community around you. Giving will propel your dream into something much bigger than you can imagine. When you are able to help someone accomplish something they couldn't do on their own, it can give wings to their dreams too.

If you think about it, giving is all about love for people and for the world around you. In the Greek language there are four types of love: eros, storge, phileo, and agape. Agape love is a selfless, sacrificial, unconditional love and is known as the highest of the four types of love in the Bible. This love is related to obedience, and it is expressed in giving. Agape love is revealed by actions not feelings. You may have great empathy for someone and feel for them, but what meets the needs of others is action. Start giving today and make an impact on someone's life.

CHAPTER SIX

Be Innovative

"Innovation distinguishes between a leader and a follower."
—Steve Jobs

America has flourished through innovation and has been built upon the hard work and creativity of inventors and entrepreneurs. In Dayton, Ohio, where I live and work, it's hard not to be inspired by the history of innovation because Dayton inventors pioneered the cash register, the yo-yo, the electric car starter, ring-pull cans, stepladder, metal ice cube tray, and, of course, human flight through the innovative minds and hands of Orville and Wilbur Wright.

You might think, *But I'm just a small business owner installing air conditioners and fixing furnaces. How innovative can I be?* Let me assure you that innovation is the key to surviving! Innovation simply means coming up with new and better ways of doing something. It means taking an old way of thinking, even something as simple as how you schedule your appointments, and figuring out how to do it better. What a thrill it is to see an innovative idea take off and work! Innovation is worth the risk of failing, worth the risk that comes with being first to bring an idea to market. Staying in the *status quo* might feel safe, but in the long term, it's the most risky way to run a business.

Being First to Market

In our attempts to be innovative, we've made lots of mistakes. We've had to adjust, tinker, and sometimes just throw out entire ideas, but we never stop there.

We've also experienced some major wins. Without an innovative spirit and willingness to be the first in our market to try new things, we would never have made the leap from a tiny start-up to a thriving, multimillion-dollar, growing business. There are several advantages to being the first to enter the market, and the chief among them are consumer impact and lack of competition.

We experienced both when we took the risk of launching after-hours service at daytime prices. Being first means you set expectations for your industry that others then have to scramble to reach. We snagged a very large amount of market share because no one else was doing it.

Companies that are first to market earn a short-term hold on that market. If they do it well, they will maintain a leading presence even after their competition enters the market. Fortunately, for us, that did not happen until five years later.

It is critical to take full advantage of that head start, for the risks of being first to market can sting. You must do it well enough to keep consumer loyalty if the market floods with competition, and it will!

Market pioneers must overcome several obstacles that their followers will not have to face. For one, they can face market ignorance. Even armed with the best research, it's difficult to know just how consumers will react to a truly innovative idea. When Henry Ford said, *"Had I asked the people what they wanted, they would've said, 'A faster horse.'"* At first, they weren't too crazy about the automobile idea. As a matter of fact, many rebelled against the change. In the April 15, 1911, issue of the *Saturday Evening Post*, there was an article titled, "Get a Horse!" It takes time for most to adapt to change. With this in mind, Steve Jobs stated, *"It's really hard to design products by focus groups. A lot of times, people don't know what they want until you show it to them."* When you are innovative, you must first show and educate the customer and then allow for a certain period of adaptation. This gives the companies who follow the luxury to base their moves on proven consumer reaction. The first to enter also takes on a considerably higher cost of innovation only to then have to worry about cheaper knockoffs.

Yes, there are risks involved, but despite these, I continue to push my company to be first to market with new ideas. When it comes to following or copying a competitor's ideas, I'd prefer not to. We will occasionally duplicate a good process and try to make it better, but most of our ideas are homegrown. As a matter of fact, the more you focus on the competition, the more you are tempted to adapt or adopt their way instead of your own, and that is dangerous. Stay original, and you'll go farther and be known as the true authority in your industry!

Fostering a Culture of Innovation

Innovation has been the ethos of our company culture. As the entrepreneur and leader, it's up to you to set the stage for a sense of adventure and freedom to encourage employees to develop and share new ideas.

As we've grown, we have been intentional with the interior design of our offices to encourage creativity. Many HVAC business offices appear to be dark, somewhat dingy and outdated, and often downright scary! At McAfee, we emphasize a clean, bright, welcoming atmosphere—what has been described as state of the art and professional.

We choose to invest in modern amenities to present a professional image and tone for our team, vendors, and customers who walk through our door. Details matter! Adequate and nicely appointed restrooms, a comfortable breakroom where employees can truly get away, and television monitors throughout the facility give our working environment a creative boost.

In our previous building, we created our own Dream Room, with sky-blue walls, red chairs, black leather couches, and even wild, bright carpet. The atmosphere puts us in a place to dream and think and be more creative and innovative. In our present facility, we have a room we call the Idea Center, with bright green, orange, and yellow walls, bright carpet, a smartboard, and a white, U-shaped table that seats twelve.

We also invested in switching the entire lighting system, both interior and exterior, to LED. It was a costly endeavor but well worth the expense to boost productivity and provide a well-lit workspace. We see payback in the form of lower utility bills and rebates from power companies. It makes a difference coming to work each day in a fun, modern environment. If you want to hire high-caliber people, you must provide a high-caliber atmosphere.

Your operation should be a place to be innovative. We make it a point to have as much up-to-date equipment as we can justify, including our phone systems, security system, video conferencing, real-time scheduling software, and face-time troubleshooting. We invest in training so our teams learn the latest methods of technical and soft skills; this helps us retain good people, and good people help us improve the bottom line.

Whether you are situated in a garage, a small building, or a skyscraper, remember that you set the standards of the company atmosphere. Even a one-man shop can have the right equipment, and the right equipment pays for itself quickly. When we worked out of the garage, we were still innovative. For instance, we chose to offer free delivery on everything. Why? Because we didn't want customers to see that we were smaller than they thought we were.

Even still, the garage was very clean and had a professional office. You can be innovative at any stage of business, but we have never been so innovative that it didn't make sense. When laptops were popular and cost $3,000 each, we didn't go out and buy one for every truck. Now that tablets do the same thing for far less, they make more sense. If you do the best you can afford to do, you can still be innovative. I sometimes hear small shop owners say, *"We turn down new customers all the time because we can't get to them."* When I hear that, I cringe and want to scream. Surely, they can and must find a way! I have no problem spending money to attract new customers, and there is no way I'd want to turn any potential clients away on purpose.

To be innovative, you have to be willing to move beyond the way things have always been. According to the late Ronald Reagan, *"Status quo, you know, that is Latin for 'the mess we're in.'"*

We long held to the idea of making sure a live person answered every incoming call on or before the second ring. In fact, it was a hard, fast rule of our office. However, we now have a phone system that automatically places the call on hold after the second ring. Our process changed, but we still expediently take care of the customer. We must be willing to bend in certain areas in order to change for the better.

CHAPTER SEVEN

Be Passionate

"Without passion, you don't have energy; without energy, you have nothing." —Donald Trump

Your relationship with your business can be like a marriage. Maybe there is not a holy matrimony, per se, but it does have every aspect of an adventure during the start-up (dating) phase. In the beginning hopefully you are passionate and energetic. You are gung-ho and just can't wait to come in each day, like a suitor clamoring for the next date. Like marriage, the business's success, as well as your own contentment, will ultimately depend upon how well you can maintain that high level of passion. During challenging times, keeping a passionate, driven attitude can largely determine whether your business survives or fails. Passion is what powers you through the grunt work, the long hours, and all those inherent risks. Passion drives you to keep coming back, trying new things, and launching new ideas. Conversely, a passionless business venture is miserable for all.

Some scholars have denigrated passion as clouding reason. They pit passion and reason against one another, with reason being the superior choice. However, research published in the *Academy of Management Review* suggests that entrepreneurial passion can be the driving force behind success.

Passion can help entrepreneurs solve problems creatively, identify new opportunities, and master challenging situations.

I've found this to be true in my business. As the owner, I set the pace for passion. At times, I've been mistaken for being upset when I have just been really excited over changing how we do something, adopting a new idea, or just taking care of a customer.

Like most people, I'm extremely passionate about the things that interest me the most. As a young boy delivering newspapers, I was passionate about my route and getting papers delivered on time.

Entrepreneurial passion isn't something that comes about because entrepreneurs are inherently disposed to it. Rather, it's because they are engaged in something they love and can relate to well.

Michael Dell, the founder and CEO of Dell, said *"Passion should be the fire that drives your life's work."* Does that fit your work description? Is it meaningful to you? It's difficult to remain passionate about something that isn't in your heart, such as a family business you never wanted to lead or a venture that seems profitable but terribly boring. Your dream must be your passion.

My son, Travis, has worked at McAfee in some capacity since he was five years old. From emptying trash and cleaning air ducts to helping out with an installation, he's been there. It was never my intention to force him into taking over the company. I want him to do whatever *he's* most passionate about. When Travis read the first version of this book during his freshman year of high school, he came to me and said, *"Dad, are you going to be disappointed if I don't come into the family business?"*

I put him at ease by saying, "Absolutely not!" I did, however, ask what he wanted to do.

Travis told me he felt called to be a teacher. He recently

received his teaching degree and now teaches middle school students while simultaneously earning his master's degree in education. He has a desire to earn his doctorate in education and someday teach teachers as a college professor. What if I would have tried to persuade or even force him into the business? Just think what the world would have missed. My daughter, Tiffany, is nine years younger than Travis; I'm looking forward to finding out what her passions will be, but right now it's neo-nursing.

Remaining passionate about your business is easier when you can identify the areas you care most about. For me, I know it's serving others, growth, and finishing well. Henry Ford quipped, *"I do not believe a man can ever leave his business. He ought to think of it by day and dream of it by night."*

Passionate About Growth

I recall a young contractor in Texas who let his fear affect his passion. He was highly motivated and wanted to grow, but he let what he didn't know get in the way of moving forward. I recall him saying he wanted to get to the next level but had never hired that many or had that many work for him before. My advice was simple: either you want to grow or you don't, but don't let fear burn out your passion. He ended up hiring two more technicians and bought two more trucks. Everything worked out well and today he will tell you that was the last time he hesitated and let fear slow him down.

Although a high percentage of trade service companies are one- or two-man shops, I knew early on that I wanted to run a bigger operation. I was passionate about growing a heating and air service company, even before I knew much about business.

Of course, my entrepreneurial passion alone did not cause my customers to start calling, but it did give me the energy to pursue growth opportunities, invest in marketing, and continually strive for improvement.

As I completed goals, my passion grew for the little things that would offer big bottom-line results, such as improving our hiring and scheduling processes. I'm passionate about reaching a certain sales goal and continuing to dominate our market. I thrive on envisioning what future growth will look like for my company—what the McAfee of ten years from now and beyond will be.

Passion must be your driving force, and it should be contagious. A passionate person attracts others, and your passion will motivate your team. If you are not excited about what you do, no one else will be either. Help your team set goals that tie directly to the growth of the business and make sure to celebrate their victories. "*Winning is a habit. Unfortunately, so is losing,*" said Vince Lombardi.

We were very passionate about making previous ideas work and prosper; the growth that came from launching them motivated us to persevere trying other novel concepts.

How can you keep your passion alive if your business isn't growing? First, don't get overwhelmed by dream killers like hopelessness and defeat. Find something you just love about it. Even when you aren't growing, you can strive to do things well. Everyone gets into a slump now and then. In basketball you are taught to just keep shooting. In business you simply have to keep looking ahead, working smart, and expecting growth. We all have our valleys to cross and mountains to go over. They say more businesses fail going up the mountain than down anyway.

A slump is the best time to evaluate yourself and your business.

Why are you in business? If you are passionate only about making money, you're going to be disappointed, because you'll be chasing that dream forever. Guy Kawasaki said, *"Great companies start because the founders want to change the world...not make a fast buck."* However, if you have a deep desire to serve others and are zealous about it, you will make the bucks.

Passionate people rarely give up, but they must know when to put a bad idea to sleep or make serious changes and adjustments. Mistakes are part of life, and I've found that the people who desire to try new things and aren't afraid of change are prone to make the most mistakes. Mistakes are best when they are admitted, learned from, and then moved on from and not repeated. In *Today Matters*, John C. Maxwell writes:

> *"For years, I kept a sign on my desk that helped me maintain the right perspective concerning yesterday. It simply said, 'Yesterday ended last night.' It reminds me that no matter how badly I might have failed in the past, it's done, and today is a new day. Conversely, no matter what goals I may have accomplished or awards I may have received, they have little direct impact on what I do today. I can't celebrate my way to success either."*

I take that to mean this: Success or failure, we should not remain stuck in the muck of either. We must keep moving!

Being passionate about growth can also help you avoid becoming satisfied or content. The worst thing for a business owner to do is to become complacent. By definition, complacency deals with being self-satisfied with your accomplishments while being unaware of potential danger. Imagine a business owner who worked years to dominate his market. He was motivated to risk more, worked overtime, took additional classes, and did whatever he had to do to reach the top. When he finally hit that pinnacle, he was overwhelmed with a sense of accomplishment and self-satisfaction. Eventually though, a young competitor, motivated and hungry, came from behind and not only caught up with him but also surpassed him, leaving him in the dust. What did that young competitor have? Passion!

If we are not careful, we can allow our accomplishments, victories, and knowledge to cause us to become satisfied in our current stage of achievement. In this way, periods of growth can threaten your passion. The fact is that many small business owners don't know how to handle growth and they let it go to their heads. They get sloppy or lazy and end up losing it all. On the other hand, they can become so busy that what was once their passion becomes a hassle rather than an opportunity. What typically happens then is they hire employees too quickly and neglect proper training. This will ultimately hurt the company, causing it to lose customers and good employees and negatively impact the business culture.

Passionate About Service

One of the hallmarks of our business is our passion for customer service. It's all about offering good service and it must radiate from you to your entire team. We just plain take care of people, meet their needs, and solve their problems. This also includes ensuring their comfort.

Our sense of urgency has always separated us from the competition. As I've already admitted more than once in this book, I've never been the most patient person, but I've taken that so-called weakness and converted it into a strength for my business. We always get to our customers as quickly as possible because I do not like to wait myself. We train our installers to complete a full installation in six to eight hours. Few people today want workers in their home for long periods. We train our customer service representatives with proper phone etiquette so customers will sense that their service call is the most important call of the day. Our service technicians carry fresh uniforms with them and are required to look just as fresh on the final call of the day as they did on the first. We don't ask our customers if they want these things; they are what we want for our customers. We know they appreciate it because they keep coming back and referring us to others. Our passion to serve is a critical ingredient to our longevity. We take care of people and we are swift about it.

Hiring passionate employees is critical when it comes to maintaining the level of customer service we expect. How can you detect true passion? Most people can feign enthusiasm in interviews, especially when they really need a job. When interviewing potential employees, we like to ask about their personal interests and hobbies. Listening to someone describe what they voluntarily put their time and effort into doing— whether it's rebuilding engines, cultivating a garden, reading, exercising, or anything else—reveals their capacity for passion. We are leery about hiring anyone with no interests. A good friend of mine, evangelist Robert W. Taylor, used to say, *"If you list everything a person thinks about in a day, you can tell what kind of a person they are."* A person who cares about nothing in their personal life is likely to care about little at work. The best time to find that out is before you hire them.

An Important Lesson in Customer Service Comes Full Circle

Early in our business, we sold a system to Vito U., the general manager of a local cafeteria. I told him we would arrive at his home at 8:00 a.m. for his installation. For some odd reason, we were running late and arrived at 8:15. I knocked on his door and received no answer, so I assumed he wasn't home.

Seconds later he appeared at the door and greeted me with a cold stare and a warning: *"If you were in the restaurant business, you would be out of business."*

"Excuse me?" I said.

He continued, *"In order for us to open at eight, we have to come in at five. I guess I just expected you here on time."*

I was taken aback by his actions and remarks, but I never forgot his words. From that point on, we guaranteed that our first appointment of the day—and any other appointments we could control—would begin on time, right down to the minute. I realized how important that was for him and for every other customer. We don't arrive early or late. Arriving ten minutes early can throw off the schedule of a parent getting kids ready for school. You have to be on time, plain and simple. I had always been concerned about being on time for a job, but until that moment, I didn't realize how important it was to be there at exactly the right time. It became an important principle of our business, and we do not waver from it today.

Funny story: Twenty-five years later, after Vito had long moved on and other successors took his place, we hired his cafeteria to cater our company breakfast. Unbelievably, they were late!

Passionate About Finishing Well

Projects left unfinished are a burden on someone's shoulders—often someone else's because they have to bat cleanup. Isn't it an awful feeling of disappointment to leave something undone? An unfinished project can zap energy and passion. We must be vigorous about completing things, no matter how big or small the task. It's critical for us to finish every installation in that six- to eight-hour time period, which exceeds industry standards. It takes passion to set lofty goals, but accomplishing those goals tends to produce even more passion. When we arrive at an installation, we must quickly design a system to meet our goal.

Every job is different, from the layout of the home to the layout of the system to the amount of preparation needed. Our attention to completing each job to its own specifications, in a timely manner, ties directly to the plan. We are passionate about quality work as well. Although some of our work may be hidden in a closet or basement, it matters to us what it looks like.

When we bring in new installers who have previous experience from other companies, they often wonder how installing so quickly is possible. This is why we hire and train so many right out of trade schools. It's critical that no matter where our new employees come from, they are willing to adapt to our methods; the McAfee Way.

Once our way is mastered, the next step is to continue to improve and become more efficient. We operate at a fast pace, but why shouldn't we? Customers are used to doing and having things done fast. This is why we have an installation timeline, and we hold our teams accountable for meeting them. It's not as hard as it sounds, if you teach and show them how. Again, if it's important to you, the owner, it will become important to them as well, and they will see the benefits.

Rekindling Passion

What will happen if you lose your passion? At some point, passion can falter under the pressure of running a business. Perhaps you grew too fast and couldn't keep up with the changes, or maybe business has slowed and the harsh realities of layoffs and cutbacks have left you in a depressive state. Maybe something in your personal life is draining your motivation, or you just can't keep up with everything on your agenda. You are still dedicated to your dream, but the passion that drove the will to succeed has waned. First, realize that this is okay. Many of us have experienced this or will experience something similar. Know that there is hope to rekindle and sustain passion in your business.

Some business owners claim they are content to run small shops with minimal growth. However, when I coach them, I've learned that many at that level appear to be just as stressed as those running much larger companies. After all, there is only so much one or two people can do without a team at their disposal. For many, running a one-man show or a mom-and-pop shop becomes a 24/7 endeavor leading to burnout, and the passion to make their business grow quickly fades. Running a business leaves them in a dreary, overworked routine with little to show for it.

If this sounds familiar, consider these steps:

- Make a concentrated effort to become more passionate about your business/livelihood.
- Surround yourself with passionate people.
- Read books by passionate authors such as John C. Maxwell, Ken Blanchard, Jim Collins, or Jeffrey Gitomer.

- Identify what stresses you the most in your business and set out to eliminate it. What brings you joy and happiness in business? Once you find out what it is, add more of it into your life and company.

Many business owners go through a moping period. Don't worry—so does the American bald eagle. At a certain age, this majestic bird endures a bitter state of depression. His feathers thicken and ruffle, his beak hardens with calcium deposits, and his talons dull. Eagle experts say some of the birds even lose their will to live. As is the case with so much in nature, though, an amazing thing happens: other eagles, those who've gone through such a hard time, fly over and drop fresh meat down to their moping friend, squawking encouragement to entice him to eat, take to the sky, and renew himself. Like the eagle, many business owners lose their drive and passion to be in business. When profits are low and debt is high, it takes a toll, draining the zest the business owner once had. They mistakenly think if they just make it go away, they'll feel better, and they begin to doubt whether they should be in business at all.

One of my favorite Bible verses proclaims, *"But they that wait upon the Lord shall renew their strength; they shall mount up with wings as eagles; they shall run, and not be weary; and they shall walk, and not faint."* Isaiah 40:31 (KJV)

My friend, I hope this book can be the fresh meat you need to take to the sky with your business again! Here are five ways to avoid staying in the moping period:

1. Set realistic goals.

2. Don't spend more than you make.

3. Keep changing and improving.

4. Avoid becoming too content.

5. Hang around other eagles (not turkeys).

At McAfee, the effort to improve and grow might entail adding or replacing a slogan or procedure, a uniform change, a logo update, a new technology or system, new website, software, or just a better way of doing something. Looking to the future drives me. It can drive you, too, but you have to want it and dream about it. It would be very hard for me to keep my passion intact if I lumbered into work unenthusiastically and did the same thing day in and day out.

Think about a changeup pitch in baseball. The changeup is thrown with the same arm action as a fastball but at a lower velocity due to the pitcher holding the ball in a special grip. The longtime pitching coach Leo Mazzone explains in his book, Pitch Like a Pro:

"When a pitcher throws his best fastball, he puts more in it; the changeup is such that one throws something other than his best fastball. By having this mindset, the pitch will have less velocity on it in addition to the change in grips. This difference from what is expected by the arm action and the velocity can confuse the batter into swinging the bat far too early and thus receiving a strike, or not swinging at all. Should a batter be fooled on the timing of the pitch and still make contact, it will cause a foul ball or the ball being put into play weakly, usually resulting in an out. In addition to the unexpected slow velocity, the changeup can also possess a significant amount of movement, which can bewilder the batter even further. The very best changeups utilize both deception and movement."

If the pitcher threw a fastball every time, the batter would know what to expect and have a better chance of getting a hit. Perhaps even more noteworthy, the pitcher wouldn't last long. He would throw his arm out and be forced to retire young! How does this relate to business? Simply put, don't get satisfied; change things up every so often. It will help you and your team. Make it fun!

Consider what areas of your business excite you the most. If you can't think of any, you might need to ask yourself some bigger questions: *Is this really my dream? Is this truly my passion or just something I fell into? Why am I doing this?* If you're not passionate about your dream, you won't be passionate about making it happen.

Dangerous Passions

This chapter would not be complete if I didn't touch on this subject. An old urban legend describes an encounter between a large naval ship and what appears to be another vessel with which the ship is on a collision course. The naval vessel, usually identified as the United States Navy and generally described as a battleship, requests via Morse code that the other ship change course. The other party responds that the naval vessel should change course. The captain of the naval vessel reiterates the demand, identifying himself as the ship captain, and commands the smaller vessel to move. The final response was, "You change course right now! I'm a lighthouse!"

As business owners, we are the captains of the ships; however, if we allow that to go to our heads, we can easily stray off course. It is dangerous to have unhealthy passions, like a desire for power, sex, money, substances, or more control. Many drift off course and collide because they let their position go to their heads and ignore the demands from the lighthouse. Unfortunately, many have lost everything in the process. Don't let this be you. Remember that unhealthy passions will keep you from being your best.

CHAPTER EIGHT

Be Disruptive

"Disruptive innovation is entrepreneurs changing their industry with unique creativity." —*Onyi Anyado*

Disruptions are a way of life today, and many businesses have had to close their doors because of them. Let's face it: Blockbuster didn't stand a chance when Netflix disrupted their world. In the 1960s the average Fortune 500 Company lasted up to seventy five years. Today, they are lucky to last fifteen years. That should tell you something about the necessity to disrupt.

Even Henry Ford made a few mistakes that kept his company from being even more successful and iconic in his time. As long as the Model T design remained ahead of the competition and competed on price, and as long as the market needs remained static, his was a successful and disruptive innovation strategy. Ford had no compelling reason to innovate in any sphere other than cost and price reduction, so his company remained the disruptor.

However, once other manufacturers came out with sleeker models and exciting colors (not just black), Ford Motor Company took a hit to its market share and Henry's pocketbook.

Henry was well known for saying and proving, *"Everything can always be done faster and better,"* and he was proud of the fact that the black paint his company used dried faster than any other paint in his day. What Henry failed to realize was that people were willing to pay more for variety. As we know, at times Henry really didn't care much about what the customer wanted.

What Is Disruptive Innovation?

"In business, a disruptive innovation is an innovation that creates a new market and value network and eventually disrupts an existing market and value network, displacing established market-leading firms, products, and alliances." —Wikipedia

This is my favorite chapter. I hope it's as exciting and energizing for you as it is for me. There is much to be learned in this area and very little is taught in business schools about it.

The McAfee definition of *"disruption"* is any innovative, outside-the-box idea, service, or invention that leaves any and all competitors flat out speechless. It's something so good that the first thing out of a competitor's mouth is unrepeatable, but the second thing is, *"Why didn't we think of that?"*

In his blog, Rick Warp, CEO of Clarity (get-clarity.com) shares the characteristic differences of being a disruptor and disruptee:

Characteristics of Disruptees:

- They fail to appreciate changes in the market, whether customer behaviors/expectations, technology, business models, new entrants, etc.
- They are invested heavily in status quo, with the entire company optimized to deliver what may soon be not nearly good enough.

- Their installed base demands continuity and backward compatibility.
- Old product designs are too cumbersome to move quickly without starting over.
- They don't have the needed expertise for desired changes and are unwilling to build or acquire it.
- Sacred cows and old biases flourish, affecting even the best of intentions to change.

Characteristics of Disruptors:

- They recognize the possibilities of a new reality and refuse to be slaves to the past.
- They deal with the installed base issue to regain quickness.
- They fully commit to appropriate initiatives.
- They modify their investment profiles to fit.
- Regular check-ups and adjustments keep old biases at bay.
- Critically, they are either new companies or are willing to find a way to recapture their entrepreneurial heritage.

The disruption mindset is where entrepreneurs should be spending much of their time. I didn't realize what a disruptor I had become until a good competitor shared it with me. After reviewing how and what we've disrupted over the twenty-eight years, it was obvious.

My humble kitchen table beginning without any customers was not much of a disruptive start, but a few years later, after moving into the garage and selling a million-dollar job, we conceived our first disruption. I contacted the owner and asked him what it would take to get the job. He said he wasn't quite sure, but he was concerned about whether the air conditioning units would even fit between the porches as I said they would. I assured him they would, but then after I hung up, I went one step further and picked up two units and a helper and drove to the location of the job and set up the units between the porches. There was plenty of room. I then called him and asked him if he could meet me. He pulled up, got out of his car, and just smiled and said, *"You got the job!"* Were the other bigger and well-established companies who also quoted that job asking themselves why they didn't get that job? You bet they were! That gig, replacing five hundred furnaces and adding five hundred central air units, kept us busy for over three years of consistent work and steady cash flow.

Our second disruption came a few years later when my first employee, Scott, came up with the idea of custom bending all copper tubing, which is the copper lines that carry the air conditioning refrigerant gas. Instead of having to braze in copper fittings such as elbows and couplings, we invested in a few bending tools. We then custom bent all the elbows, leaving only a few places to braze rather than several. The leak ratio of refrigerant dropped dramatically, which meant fewer expensive repairs and recalls.

You may wonder where the disruption was in Scott's brilliant procedural change. I ran all my own sales then, so you can guess what I told the customer. You got it! I was happy to say, *"We custom bend all our copper fittings, which reduces leaks substantially."* Customers who had experienced costly repairs felt the pain and went with us, perhaps for that one reason. Those who shopped around asked other companies if they did the same, and the answer was usually no. Today, most companies in our area custom bend their copper tubing.

Our third disruption came when we built an 11,000-square-foot facility in a very nice corporate area. As long as we were in that garage, we were not as big of a threat to anyone, but our new building got heads turning.

In case I have not mentioned it, there were and still are older second- and third-generation HVAC companies that have been around a long time, but are still doing things the way they've been doing them for decades, which can be a great advantage for a new company emerging into a market. It was certainly an advantage for us since we were not interested in doing business their way, but rather we chose to serve the customer better, faster, more professional, and using new methods.

Many of those older companies in our area required two to three days to install new systems in homes. Within our first few years of operation, we were able to get that down to one to two days. I knew I could improve on that. We could easily make it a one-day process by tearing out the old system; pre-measuring and ordering any duct work upon arrival of the job; and getting any sheet metal transitions delivered by noon.

We had another concern as I had mentioned in the first chapter: the sheet metal shop we contracted was not interested in keeping up with our growth. We chose to start our own sheet metal shop from scratch, and it took off strong. Because of that, we were able to make the one-day install a reality. We emphasized to our customers that we would be in and out of their homes in one day.

Today, people are much busier than ever. The faster you get in and out of their home, the happier they are. Once we mastered the one-day install, we came out with a guarantee: *"Installed in one day or I'll give you back $1,000."* Was this another disruption for my competition? You better believe it!

One of the greatest disruptions was our epic *"8:00 to 8:00, Same Great Rate™"* concept. Again, this ultimately caused hundreds of my competitors to say words I cannot repeat here, left them shaking and scratching their heads and asking why they didn't think of it first. Initially, they seemed a bit inactive and lethargic about it, because none of them really wanted to up their game; they just hoped and prayed it would fail and go away. Of course, after five years of heavy marketing, no one came up with anything better. In our area, it was more than just a disruption. It was staggering. We knew it and capitalized on it. We took more market share over that five-year period than any other time in our company's history.

Finally, after about the seventh year, several companies attempted to offer after-hours service at the same rate. However, and this is very important, you did not find us sitting in a conference room or in the Idea Center figuring out how to improve on our *"8:00 to 8:00, Same Great Rate."* Being the disruptor, we stayed a step ahead and came up with the *"Any Season, Any Time™"* campaign. We hit the ground running with high-caliber TV commercials. We are *"a 24/7/365 Emergency Residential HVAC company with service on demand."* If *"Any Season, Any Time™"* doesn't describe us, I'm not sure what does.

Even better, once we changed our campaign, our competitors' ads for after-hour services dissipated. To stay ahead of the rest, we now invest hundreds of thousands in TV and radio commercials. Many of them can be seen at www.mcair.com. Our TV spots make it clear that we are not the norm in the HVAC industry; we disrupt in many demographics. How many local HVAC companies hire a production company to produce ads of national quality? We make it hard to compete with us because we know where and how to buy media. This more expensive, high-caliber advertising was not possible in our first or even second decade of business.

Today, though, because of increased revenue and minimal debt, we have freedom and can do what other companies cannot.

For years, we asked our customers if they needed furnace filters so we could deliver them during service calls. Too often, we took the wrong filters, damaged filters, or just forgot them altogether. This did not help our image, and we were losing money having to return to those homes with the correct product. We decided to eliminate this problem by implementing our own online filter delivery service. McAfee Filters (www.mcafeefilters. com) are manufactured right here in Ohio and delivered free.

At times, we don't set out to disrupt, per se. We just work hard and think of ways to serve our customers better and faster. Many of the ideas naturally become disruptions, which become difficult to compete with. When that happens, it's an exhilarating feeling to push ourselves to dominate the market. Some companies blindly allow success to breed complacency and complacency to breed failure. Realizing that, we do not allow ourselves to become satisfied. Rather, we have to celebrate all wins but quickly move on to the next contest.

How to Bring Disruption to Your Company

I want to share how you too can learn to disrupt your territory or even your entire industry. First, we all know the word *active* means doing something, but placing just a few letters in front of that word shows us four ways we can act.

Reactive. Many companies just react to whatever comes their way. In the HVAC business, that might involve the weather.

Most reactive business owners fear the future and would love to turn back the clock and return to the *"good ole' days."* There is nothing wrong with looking back fondly on the past, but what are you going to do today and tomorrow?

Inactive. Being inactive means a desire to freeze the present and hope for no change. Maybe the past was a nightmare, so it is hard to see hope in the future. Maybe there has been too much change, and you're just not sure how to handle it. Maybe it has to do with John Maxwell's Law of the Lid, which he discusses on his blog

> *I often open my leadership conferences by explaining the Law of the Lid because it helps people understand the value of leadership. If you can get a handle on this law, you will see the incredible impact of leadership on every aspect of life. So here it is: leadership ability is the lid that determines a person's level of effectiveness. The lower an individual's ability to lead, the lower the lid on his potential. The higher the individual's ability to lead, the higher the lid on his potential. To give you an example, if your leadership rates an 8, then your effectiveness can never be greater than a 7. If your leadership is only a 4, then your effectiveness will be no higher than a 3. Your leadership ability—for better or for worse—always determines your effectiveness and the potential impact of your organization.*

We all have a lid rating, some higher than others. Many who are inactive seem to fall in the lower lid ratings. They remind me of Eeyore from Winnie the Pooh—just pessimistic, gloomy, negative, and stubbornly opposed to taking risks. Could this be why they remain in the lower of the lid ratings?

Pre-active. This type of response is not well known, it means being creative and solving problems before they become problems. A pre-active person attempts to predict the future and then plan for it. Way before most HVAC companies in our area realized what was happening; we created a future out of the garage. The US EPA Clean Air Act, Title VI, Section 608 changed the rules on venting refrigerant gas into the atmosphere. Right or wrong, we used to let the gas escape during an installation of a new system or while performing certain services. As soon as we could, we invested in recovering machines and became certified in installing the new refrigerant R410a system years before our competition. We were pre-active because we took advantage of the difficult situation we all found ourselves in.

Another strong sales technique we used while selling an air conditioner or heat pump: I would ask, *"Would you prefer the old type with Freon or the new model with environmentally sound refrigerant?"* Eight out of ten preferred the new. If they did seek other estimates, and those companies did not find it important to quote the new equipment, it definitely brought up questions. We were the first in Dayton to install the new environmentally sound units.

Proactive. Being proactive is to make things happen instead of waiting for them to happen. As I mentioned in previous chapters, we private label all HVAC systems we sell. However, when we first started the planning process, I was first pre-active in my planning. I predicted that placing my trusted name on our equipment would assure our customers that the already well-known and dependable name of McAfee would help us sell more systems and retain those customers for all their future service. Once that plan was in place, we became proactive by meeting with several manufacturers to see who would like my name on their equipment.

This is good to know if you are considering private labeling: Not every manufacturer says yes. My proactive plan was to first find a manufacturer, and with help from a supplier, I did. Second, I wanted to brand it so well that people would buy a McAfee System over a national brand. As expected, that took time, but we have created a high-quality, trusted brand name.

Being proactive also means we can shape and control the outcome of the plan. Never tell a true entrepreneur that they can't create the future, because this is exactly what we did with the McAfee System. After eleven years of private labeling, we conducted a survey that was fielded via the internet using an independent panel supplied by Bernett Research.

We had 451 people complete the study, which measured brand awareness and perceptions of HVAC companies. The participants were adults ages twenty-five to seventy-four who owned homes and lived in the Dayton metro (as defined by county). According to that survey and several others since then, the McAfee brand was top of mind in the residential HVAC brands in our territory, outranking very large companies with well-known name brands such as Carrier, Bryant, and Goodman. As proactive as we were with our marketing and branding, those results got us excited to see just what kind of disruptions we were creating.

For many years the standard warranty on a new residential HVAC system was twenty years on heat exchangers, ten years on compressors, and one year on parts and labor. I had so much confidence in the quality of our installations that I decided to offer as standard, a seven-year parts and labor warranty on all McAfee Systems. Granted, anyone can buy extended warranties with more coverage, but ours came standard. This was another disruption in our territory. Even today, other companies simply find it hard to compete.

If you want to disrupt your territory, go back to Chapter 1 and study strategy. If I had just stopped at the memory of selling a million-dollar job, being the first to sell environmentally sound equipment, or even moving into a professional facility, where would we be today?

Stay Ready, Stay Current

The longer you are in business, the more you will realize the necessity for change. While your marketing message may stay the same, the methods of appealing to and reaching existing and new customers will differ. Leading businesses stay current, whether it's understanding the latest technology or figuring out what drives various generations of consumers. According to futurist Daniel Burrus, *"It used to be that the big ate the small. Now, the fast eat the slow."* If you do not plan for change, you will change by default. Our brand, serving others fast, has changed sooner and quicker than that of our competition, and this has paid off well for us.

The size of the company no longer defines its success; rather, it is that company's ability to react quickly to changes. Your competitive advantage depends on the ability to move rapidly and decisively in responding to customers and employees.

We all know HVAC systems will continue to increase in efficiency, but can a gas furnace ever reach 100 percent efficiency? We are only a few percentage points away from it as I write this book. Do you foresee your utility company crediting your account for the amount saved? This may be doubtful, but central air and heat pumps still have room to climb in efficiency, and let us not forget that solar is still improving. We also know that the smart thermostat, smart gas valve, and smart home will only be getting smarter. That is a hard trend for sure, but one we should be focusing on.

Today, I can push a button, and a box of goods will be delivered tomorrow. Do you think your customer wants and expects that kind of quick service from you? What happens when they call you and they hear, we can be there in two days or two weeks? Worse yet, what if they call and get only a voicemail?

Ayn Rand was right when she said, *"Anyone who fights for the future, lives in it today."* It's hard to make adjustments for tomorrow if you are not living it. Your tomorrow will only be different if you start changing your today. What got you here won't get you there. As you go about your day in *status quo* mode, one of your competitors is figuring out ways to serve people better and more quickly than you do.

Isaac University

My friend Ray Isaac of Isaac Heating and Air Conditioning located in Rochester has truly disrupted his territory of upstate New York and probably New York itself. As one of the nation's largest privately held heating, ventilation, and air conditioning contractors, the Isaac team has shaken our industry both in how an HVAC company operates and in how they think. The company, which now has over 370 employees, provides residential, commercial, and industrial service and installation, as well as home performance, home services, plumbing, electrical, and carpentry. From its humble beginning in 1945, Isaac can now claim annual revenues over $52 million. As is the case for most HVAC companies, Ray and his team found it tough to find skilled applicants. Instead of just complaining, in 2001, they founded the accredited Isaac University (IU). The program is just for Isaac employees, and hundreds attend every year. Currently, Isaac Heating invests close to a million dollars in training and education. Through Isaac University, they also conduct several boot camps annually, consisting of a paid twelve-week training and education program that builds technicians from the ground up. Isaac is now strategizing on how to take their IU program to even higher levels, further disrupting the market and gaining a competitive advantage in the talent market and labor pool.

If you're an HVAC contractor in Upstate New York doing your best to compete with Isaac, then discover they sponsor an accredited HVAC technical training university that promises students positions within their company? As with most disruptions, you just shake your head.

Awards Won

As I mentioned, we are a recipient of the prestigious BBB Torch Award. This award represents the legacy of great Miami Valley, Ohio business pioneers such as John Patterson, Wilbur and Orville Wright, Charles Kettering, Colonel Edward Deeds, and, most recently, Clay Mathile, previous owner of IAMS Pet Food. It has been through their ingenuity, leadership, generosity, and mentorship to others that the Miami Valley has withstood the test of time and re-created itself again and again. Of all the accolades we've been granted, this one stands out, but as mentioned, we celebrated, mounted the trophy and moved on.

CHAPTER NINE

Be Ready

"Before everything else, getting ready is the secret of success."
—Henry Ford

You might be sitting in your garage, home office, or even your kitchen, wondering if growth can really come to you today. It can! Just think: It wasn't so long ago that my wife and I were sitting at our humble kitchen table paying company bills. It wasn't so long ago that I was staring at my back yard, strategizing where I'd build a garage/office. It wasn't so long ago I was sitting across from an empty lot, dreaming of the corporate headquarters we would someday build. Only a few years ago I purchased a 30,000-square-foot corporate headquarters building, renovated it from end to end, and sold all other buildings getting all operations back under one roof.

We have created a strong small business by implementing the principles I've shared in this book. If I can do it, you can too—if you want it. In fact, your biggest concern shouldn't be *whether* you can grow but how to handle it when you *do*.

If you implement the nine principles in this book, I'm convinced your personal and business life will change. We've grown 35,000 times since conception! We've touched on how to be strategic, be teachable, be a coach, be known, be giving, be innovative, be passionate, and be disruptive. It's a potent combination for success! I've experienced it, and I hope you will too. That's why I want to encourage you to Be Ready.

"Ready for what?" you ask. Be ready for growth and for an incredible ride. If you forge ahead with these principles, be prepared for change to come about, but again, you must want it!

Let's review:

Be strategic. No dream, no matter how small or audacious, will come to life without a strategy. Find time to dream and plan, get the right people at the board table to help you, and continually update and refer to your plan to stay on track for your dream.

Be teachable. To grow as a leader, you must be teachable. Read the best books, take good classes, and spend time with business leaders who have grown their businesses.

Most important of all, put together a board of competent, wise, capable, and trustworthy advisors for your business. The advice you receive and the accountability they provide is priceless.

Be a leader. Are you a manager or a leader? Leaders step back and see the entire field; they then empower others on their team to manage and work in their own ways while still carrying out the team's values and mission.

Be known. Spending money on advertising, branding, and marketing is a necessary risk if you want to lead in your market. If someone is going to use your service, they have to know your name.

Be giving. Aside from just being the right thing to do, building a giving culture in your business can have many practical benefits, such as employee engagement, stronger brand perception, and customer loyalty.

Be innovative. Innovation simply means coming up with new and better ways of doing something. How long have you done the same old thing day after day, expecting different results? Innovation is critical to your long-term success.

Be passionate. Before you can be motivated, you must have passion! Passion is the fuel that inspires us to act; it makes life worth living. Our passion is about who we are; our dreams are about what we want to become. Get excited about both!

Be disruptive. Think about how you can serve your customers better, faster, and with creativity. Start with small things that make a difference, and you'll experience results.

Don't be afraid of the bigger companies in your market. David took down Goliath with one stone using a sling. Sometimes being the disruptor is as simple as doing it better, faster, and with less.

And Now, We Must Be Ready

Three decades ago, I took a huge risk in leaving the life I knew to follow my dream of being a business owner. With the right approach, our growth eventually came in swift order, but it didn't catch us off guard. We were ready and able to ride each step to the next level. As Alexander Graham Bell quipped, *"Before anything else, preparation is the key to success."*

The best way to manage growth is to go back to the first principle of this book: Be strategic. Devise a strong plan, one that includes specifics about what your business will need to do to move to the next level of revenue and then be ready to tackle each level.

Be ready to risk more. You have to risk more capital to hire more people, to buy more trucks, better equipment, and one day, even a bigger facility. Risk is part of business, and it scares some people to death. Those kinds of people would rather stay a small company, but for many entrepreneurs, myself included, it can be both exciting and adventurous.

Be ready to spend your time wisely. Have a plan for your time. Today, mine is spent on teaching, growing others, and creating a better future. As you grow, revisit the chapter on leadership.

You need to figure out what others on your team should be doing to allow you to focus your time doing what you do best. In other words, if someone else can do a certain task, they should be tasked with it. Be ready for the freedom of what systems in place do. Dream more, set the vision, and grow your business. A mentor, Dave Sullivan, says, *"An entrepreneur should be employed from the neck up."* In other words, quit touching things and use your mind to think and grow your business.

Be ready for the next dream! As I've mentioned, I avoid becoming satisfied and enjoy looking for the next challenge. For now, I'm continually pushing to remain a market leader, and I'm always on the lookout for new ways to help other entrepreneurs grow. This is precisely why I updated this book. So, what is next for you?

I remember driving to Dayton Firestone as a nineteen-year-old, thinking I was heading for the best opportunity of my life. I couldn't have guessed how differently the next thirty-six years would unfold, but it was all done by visualizing one dream at a time and then pursuing it. I can't wait to hear how you are doing the same. Feel free to contact me at greg@gregmcafee.com to share your story.

The Open Book
Game of Business

TRAIN YOUR HVAC TEAM
With TOBGOB: The Open-Book Game Of Business

TOBGOB® is an innovative board game HVAC entrepreneurs can use to teach their teams how to act like entrepreneurs, boosting productivity in the process. Through four rounds of play, you have the opportunity to introduce the principles of "open-book management" to your HVAC business. TOBGOB is a great, entertaining, and educational way for individuals or teams to build camaraderie and ownership.

Think of how much fun you had playing games while you were growing up. Nothing helps bring a group into new awareness and connectedness like a board game. TOBGOB acts as a creative exercise for educational intervention. It makes learning fun and accessible! The objective of TOBGOB is to help HVAC staff members understand how their actions affect the financial success of the company.

Order today at www.tobgob.com

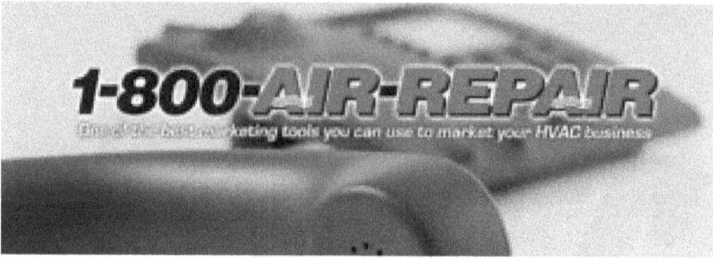

A MARKETING PLAN
THAT SETS YOUR HVAC BUSINESS APART

More than a memorable phone number, 1-800-AIR-REPAIR can be a marketing cornerstone for your heating, air conditioning, or air duct cleaning business. This subscription vanity number is exclusively assigned to geographic marketing areas in the United States. Leads and sales calls from your area code are routed directly to you, 24 hours a day, 7 days a week, 365 days a year.

With our exclusive marketing support system and your investment of time, your business can grow to exceed your expectations, and you can make your dream of a successful, profitable organization a reality. Don't wait...and don't miss another opportunity for a sale! Reserve your area code now at:

www.1-800-air-repair.com

Resources and Works Cited

Aileron. http://www.aileron.org/.

Allen, Scott. "Henry Ford: Founder of Ford Motor Company and Assembly Line Innovator." http://entrepreneurs.about. com/od/famousentrepreneurs/p/henryford.htm.

American Marketing Association. "Definition of Marketing." http://www.marketingpower.com/AboutAMA/Pages/ Definitionof Marketing.aspx.

Better Business Bureau. "Small Business Charitable Giving Guide for the Holiday Season." 31 October 2007. http://www. bbb.org/us/article/small-business-charitable-giving- guide-for- the-holiday-season-1907.

Blanchard, Ken, The Ken Blanchard Companies. http://www. kenblanchard.com/.

Bowman, Jim, Rexarc International, Inc. http://www.rexarc. com/.

Burkett, Larry. *Business by the Book.* Thomas Nelson Publishers, 2003. Cardon, M. S., J. Wincent, J. Singh, and M. Drnovsek. "The Nature and Experience of Entrepreneurial Passion." *Academy of Management Review*, 2009.

Buzzwell, Dr. Sid, General Editor. *Leadership Bible.* Zondervan Publishing House.

"Changeup." Wikipedia, modified 17 September 2011. http://en.wikipedia.org/wiki/Changeup.

Chick-fil-A Inc. "Fast Facts." http://www.truettcathy.com/ pdfs/CFAFastFacts.pdf .

City of Dayton. "Dayton Inventions." http://www.daytonohio. gov/departments/pa/Pages/inventionlist.aspx.

Coca-Cola. http://www.coca-cola.com/en/index.html. Collins, Jim. http://www.jimcollins.com/.

Dell, Michael S. "Michael S. Dell Keynote Address," The University of Texas at Austin, 2003. http://www.utexas.edu/ commencement/2003/spring/speech.html.

Deloitte LLP. "2004 Deloitte Volunteer IMPACT Survey." http://www.deloitte.com/view/en_US/us/About/Community-Involvement/039d899a961fb110VgnVCM100000ba42f00aR CRD. htm.

Disney, Walt. Disney Institute, Nicole Lauria, November 3, 2009. CRM Magazine by Christopher Musico, contributor.

"Donald Trump." Wikiquote, modified 28 August 2011. http://en.wikiquote.org/wiki/Donald_Trump.

Edison, Thomas. http://www.brainyquote.com/quotes/quotes/t/thomasaed136875.ht ml.

Entrepreneur.com. "Small Business Encyclopedia: Branding." http://www.entrepreneur.com/encyclopedia/term/82248.html.

Ford, Henry. http://www.quotedb.com/quotes/2094.

Etzell, W. Theodore III. Conditioned Air. http://www.conditionedair.com

Foreman, George. George Foreman Electric Grills. http:// www.georgeforemancooking.com/.

Frankl, Viktor E. *Man's Search for Meaning.* Pocket Books, 1946;1997. Gitomer, Jeffery. http://www.gitomer.com/.

Grunkemeyer, Mark. Buckeye Ecocare, Centerville, Ohio. http://www.buckeyeecocare.com/about/.

Hersey, Paul and Ken Blanchard. *Management of Organizational Behavior.* Prentice Hall, 2011.

Hobaica, Louis. Hobaica Services Inc., Phoenix, Arizona. http://www.hobaica.com/.

Holy Bible (King James, New King James, and New International Versions): Isaiah 40:31; Proverbs 19:20; and Exodus 18:13–26.

Humphrey, Albert. "Stakeholders Concept and SWOT Analysis," Stanford University, 1960–70.

Isaac, Ray. Isaac Heating. http://www.isaacheating.com

Jobs, Steve. http://thinkexist.com/quotation/innovation-distinguishes- between-a-leader-and-a/392765.html.

Landry, Tom. http://humanresources.about.com/od/workrelationships/a/quotes_l eaders.htm.

Lim, Terence, PhD. "Social Impact, Business Benefits, and Investor Returns." Committee Encouraging Corporate Philanthropy, 2009. http://www.corporatephilanthropy.org/pdfs/resources/MVCP_repo rt_singles.pdf.

Lombardi, Vince. http://www.vincelombardi.com/.

Mathile, Clay. http://business.uc.edu/centers/goering/educational- programs/business-institute.html.

Maxwell, John C. The Maxwell Leadership Bible (New King James Version). Thomas Nelson Publishers, 2002.

Maxwell, John C. Today Matters: *12 Daily Practices to Guarantee Tomorrow's Success.* Center Street, 2004.

Mays, Benjamin. http://www.morehouse.edu/about/chapel/mays_wisdom.html.

McAfee Foundation for Children and Youth, in Partnership with Dayton Children's. http://www.mcafeefoundation.com/makeadifference.htm.

McAfee, Greg. Greg McAfee Resources for HVAC Business Success. "A Marketing Plan that Sets Your HVAC Business Apart." http://www.1-800-air-repair.com/.

McAfee, Greg. Greg McAfee Resources for HVAC Business Success. "Train Your HVAC Team with the Open Book Game of Business: TOBGOB." http://www.tobgob.com/.

Minor & Brown PC, Attorneys and Counselors, Denver, Colorado. http://www.minorbrown.com/about-us/.

Musico, Christopher. "Brand Lessons Learned from Mickey Mouse." Destination CRM, 3 November 2009. http://www. destinationcrm.com/Articles/CRM-News/Daily- News/Brand-Lessons-Learned-from-Mickey-Mouse-57620.aspx.

Nike. http://www.nikebiz.com/?sitesrc=uslp.

"Quotes/Ronald Reagan." Wikipedia, modified 19 February 2008. http://www.dkosopedia.com/wiki/Quotes/Ronald_Reagan.

Redenbacher, Orville. Orville Redenbacher's Gourmet Popping Corn. http://www.orville.com/about-us/history.jsp.

Rogers, Will. http://www.leadershipnow.com/initiativequotes. html.

Rosenthal, Jim and Leo Mazzone. *Pitch Like a Pro: A Guide for Young Pitchers and Their Coaches, Little League through High School.* St. Martin's Griffin, 1999.

Rothschild, William E. http://mysite.verizon.net/vzesz4a6/current/id317.html.

Seuss, Dr. *Happy Birthday To You!* Random House Children's Books, 2003.

Swepston, Mark. Atlas Butler Heating. http://www.atlasbutler.com

Target Corporation. "Corporate Responsibility Report 2007." http://sites.target.com/images/corporate/about/responsibility_repor t/responsibility_report_social.pdf.

Thomas, Dave. Wendy's Restaurants. http://www.wendys.com/dave/.

Tucker, Preston. "The Tucker Automobile Club of America."
http://www.tuckerclub.org/.

United States Congress. "American Recovery and
Reinvestment Act of 2009."
http://www.recovery.gov/About/ Pages/The_Act.aspx.

United States Department of Commerce. Washington, DC.
http://www.commerce.gov/.

VARtek K–12 Managed Technology, Dayton, Ohio.
http:// www.vartek.com/.

Warp, Rick. Found and CEO of Clarity. http://get-clarity.com.

Wesley, John. http://quotationsbook.com/quote/27221/.

About the Author

Greg McAfee

A true entrepreneur, Greg McAfee has a passion for helping fellow HVAC business owners take their businesses to new heights. In 1990 Greg started McAfee Heating and Air with $274 and a used truck. Today Greg runs one of the most successful HVAC companies in the Midwest and is called upon to share his expertise with other business owners all over the United States. Greg is the inventor of the business game TOBGOB, an innovative board game entrepreneurs use to teach their teams how to act like entrepreneurs and boost productivity in the process. Greg McAfee's company, McAfee Heating and Air has soared from number 489 to number 1 in their residential market.

Greg has passion in all he does. As a Christian businessman, his decisions and principles are spiritually based. As a proud veteran of the US Marine Corps, Greg cares about people. Whether he is working with a HVAC business owner in Denver, Colorado, inspiring his team to take care of the customer, or following his kids' pursuits, Greg is devoted and committed.

He gets results and that's exactly what he'll do for you. Nothing gets him more excited than to talk to a HVAC business owner who isn't happy with status quo but has a passion to grow business.

You can contact Greg at: greg@gregmcafee.com.